GUARDSMAN
AND
COMMANDO

GUARDSMAN AND COMMANDO

*The War Memoirs
of RSM Cyril Feebery,* DCM

*as told to
David Feebery*

Pen & Sword
MILITARY

First published in Great Britain in 2008 by
Pen & Sword Military
An imprint of
Pen & Sword Books Ltd
47 Church Street
Barnsley
South Yorkshire
S70 2AS

Printed and bound in England
by CPI UK

Typeset by Phoenix Typesetting,
Auldgirth, Dumfriesshire

Pen & Sword Books Ltd incorporates the Imprints of Pen & Sword
Aviation, Pen & Sword Family History, Pen & Sword Maritime,
Pen & Sword Military, Wharncliffe Local History, Pen & Sword Select,
Pen & Sword Military Classics, Leo Cooper, Remember When, Seaforth
Publishing and Frontline Publishing

For a complete list of Pen & Sword titles please contact
PEN & SWORD BOOKS LIMITED
47 Church Street, Barnsley, South Yorkshire, S70 2AS, England
E-mail: enquiries@pen-and-sword.co.uk
Website: www.pen-and-sword.co.uk

Contents

Foreword

Uncle Cyril was a skilful raconteur, who loved to tell his tales about how, as he would put it, 'I won the war single handed!' I can remember, as a child at family gatherings, sitting very quietly with the grown-ups and long after my bedtime, listening spell-bound and hoping against hope that no one would notice I was still there before he reached the end of that partic-ular story. The later realisation that they weren't just made-up tales, that he really had done all those brave things, came with an enormous sense of pride that this man was my Uncle.

When my cousin Heather came from Australia to spend Christmas and New Year with us in 1993, she presented Cyril with what must by then have been a unique audience – a relative who had never heard any of his stories before. As he gave her a sort of guided tour of the action highlights, it struck me that this was the first time I had ever heard him recount his whole career consecutively from beginning to end. When Cyril later confided that his memory for names and dates and places was getting hazy and beginning to let him down, I offered to work with him to put his story on paper.

That is how this came to be written. We got together a few times over the following months, when he would talk and I would make notes and ask questions. Draft passages were posted backwards and forwards, annotated, corrected, and redrafted until we arrived at a version that finally met his exacting, his Grenadier Guards, standards.

It was meant to be an *aide-mémoire* for him as much as an historical document, but it serves both purposes. In preparing it to be published I have added some factual details and some historical background here and there, but apart from these small intrusions this remains Cyril Feebery's own story in his own words. He took great delight from leafing through it in his later years; I hope you will take as much pleasure from it now.

David Feebery
Sheffield, 2008

Chapter One

The Beginning

I enlisted in the Grenadier Guards on 20 May 1937, a few weeks after my eighteenth birthday, because I fell out with my brother.

We lived in the top floor flat of a Working Men's club in Enmore Road, South Norwood, London, where our Dad was steward. He had been a professional footballer, captain of Crystal Palace for five years until he was forced to retire through injury. As a keen sportsman himself he had always encouraged us, and we both enjoyed cycling, running and swimming. Our favourite sport was boxing. Bert was five years older than me and he joined Croydon boxing club when he was thirteen. He used to practise on me at home so I joined the club as soon as they would let me, mostly to get my own back. Bert was a qualified carpenter, but at the time of our bust-up he was boxing professionally at middleweight and doing very well. We trained and sparred together and although I was boxing at heavyweight by the age of seventeen we were a good match for each other.

Dad put up the money for Bert to buy a car, a Standard Eight, which he was paying back week by week. I was working for a furniture dealer at the time, driving his lorry even though I was so young (the rules about driving were different in those days) and I considered myself every bit as good a driver as Bert. Knowing what we were like, Dad sat us down and spelled out the conditions, one of which was that I could use the car, by arrangement with Bert, provided I paid for the petrol. That seemed fair and we shook on it.

It came to blows, as it was bound to do really, when I wanted to take a girl to the pictures in maximum style. I am certain even now that this had all been arranged, but when the time came Bert wouldn't let me use the car. It was very much his baby, and the keys stayed in his pocket. The fight started in the kitchen of the flat and ended on the doorstep three floors down, leaving a trail of wreckage all the way. No gloves this time, no sparring. We both meant it. Mum and Dad and some of the club members pulled us apart and tried to sort it out but by then I had had enough. There were bitter words in the street and I stormed off, caught the next train to central London and slept rough for a couple of nights. A typical only just eighteen year-old, I wandered around feeling very hard done by, not knowing what to do next but far too obstinate to just go home and face the music.

I had always wanted to join the RAF. The Sergeant in the Aldwych recruiting office must have had a shrewd idea of what was going on. He told me to go away and talk it over with my parents, then asked if I had any money. I had a few bob left from what I was going to spend on that girl at the pictures but told him I was broke. He gave me half a crown, saying I could repay him when I came back. I guess he knew he'd never see it again.

The idea of joining up was a good one, I thought, so I tried the Navy next. They were only interested in qualified tradesmen, but the Petty Officer looked me up and down and told me the Army were crying out for big lads like me. I thought it over during another night in the Red Shield Salvation Army hostel, then showed up at the Army recruiting office next morning. I shall never forget that Sergeant's face as I walked in. I was six foot three and still growing, and within half an hour he had convinced me that my shining future lay with the Brigade of Guards. I signed, took the King's shilling and pocketed a travel warrant to Caterham Barracks.

Then I went home. I had been away a week without a word to anyone about where I was. Mum and Dad, and Bert in his own way, had been frantic. When I turned up out of the blue having joined the Army, things went from bad to worse. There was a lot of tearful talk from Mum, and Dad was all set to buy me out. Bert even said sorry, something he found as difficult to do as I did, but it was too late. I had signed up and in a funny sort of way I was beginning to look forward to it. Next morning, with some misgivings but not many, I set off for Caterham and the welcoming smile of Corporal Walker at the Brigade of Guards Depot for Recruit Training.

It must already be clear that I was not the most docile and obedient person on earth. Even so, I learned how to stand up straight and march in step and lay out my kit for inspection. I also learned just how many things there are in the Army that need either polishing or painting white. But I was prepared to put up with all this for the sake of the sports. I joined the boxing team, the swimming team, the water polo team and the cross-country team, and loved every minute of it. I thought I was fit when I joined up, but after a few months I knew what it felt like to be really fit.

My squad passed out at the end of October and I was posted to the 3rd Battalion Grenadier Guards at Victoria Barracks, Windsor. On arrival, full of ourselves of course, we were told in no uncertain terms by Regimental Sergeant Major Turner that our troubles had only just begun. As far as he was concerned, he said, we were still recruits and he was going to knock us into shape if it killed us. It nearly did. It was drill parades and more drill parades. We all picked up punishment parades as well for the usual earth-shattering Army reasons: mug handle misaligned at kit inspection, blankets improperly folded. Even on punishment parades you could lose your good name: 'filthy' boots because you had stepped in a puddle on the way to the parade ground, 'dirty' brasses because you had come out of a warm barrack room into the cold and the shine had dulled. It took a lot for me to stand still while some sawn-off Second Lieutenant told me my cap badge was a disgrace, when he needed a step ladder to see it.

This was the hardest time so far. You grit your teeth and get on with it until it dawns on you that all this hounding is part of a process that makes sense. It's not just a matter of whether you can take it but whether you can learn from it. You never stop grousing, of course, but you begin to think things out, to get a step ahead by playing them at their own game and getting it right first time. When the old sweats see you are fighting back, they take pity and put you straight, then everybody starts working together. Within a few weeks I was beginning to feel like a Guardsman in Number One platoon, Number One Company because I was getting it right more often than not.

I kept up with the sports. The boxing and cross-country teams paraded every morning at six to run through the town to Windsor Great Park, then up the Long Walk to the Copper Horse for twenty minutes PT before breakfast. Then it was 'GIT ON PARADE!', every day, all day, practice and more practice: slow and quick marching, mounting and changing guard, trooping the colour. Midmorning break and sprint for the NAAFI, then more of the same plus arms drill and rifle inspection. We all had to be proficient in firing our rifles, of course, and we were also trained to use Lewis machine guns and Mills bombs.

These months at Windsor were spent mounting Barrack Guard and Castle Guard, and Guards of Honour for visiting dignitaries, as well as regular route marches. The Battalion took part in the Aldershot Tattoo in 1938. When the King and Queen were in residence there were

5

double guards at all posts. The first time I was on Royal Guard was with my pal Tip Tippler on the Terrace Post. Around nine in the morning a voice whispered in my ear, 'Stand by, the King is about to come out on to the terrace!' I panicked quietly until the same voice said, 'Up, sentry!' I rapped my rifle butt three times on the paving to signal Tip, then we came to the slope and the present arms in perfect time, pretty good even if I say it myself. As the King strolled past he said, 'Good morning, sentry,' as did the Queen and both princesses. We came back to the slope, and when our relief marched up the royal family stayed to watch the change. Apparently the bloke who warned me was the Police bodyguard, but I never saw him.

The Battalion moved to Aldershot, and while we were there my Company was 'relieved for public duties'. This meant that we lived at Chelsea Barracks and mounted guard at Buckingham Palace and St James Palace. Back at Aldershot again there were field exercises and training. It wasn't such a bad life. By now I was boxing for the Grenadier Guards team in amateur contests all over the country. Our tour of Ireland was very successful. I remember walking back to Chelsea Barracks after one match, with the offer of a job in the City of London Police after my time was up in the Army. I could see myself as a copper. It was all falling nicely into place when Chamberlain flew home from Munich with 'Peace in our time'.

Some hopes. I might have to start taking this soldiering business seriously after all. Reserve soldiers began to turn up, called back to the colours. Some of them had been there and done it all during the First World War, which we were still calling the Great War at the time. After a few beers they liked nothing better than telling us young lads exactly what we were in for, spinning yarns that made your hair curl. New equipment arrived too. We swapped our Lewis guns for Brens and learned how to use them. Nippy little tracked vehicles called Bren Carriers began buzzing around. Volunteers for the Army driving course were called for and I was up at the front of the queue. I could already drive, but if the Army wanted to teach me all over again on a brand new truck it was fine by me. It was a lot better than walking everywhere.

I listened to Chamberlain's speech on Sunday 3 September in the NAAFI at Barossa Barracks, Aldershot. We were all crowded in to hear it but there was none of the usual laughter and rude jokes. By the time he'd finished, all the drill and boxing and spit and polish seemed pointless, part of another world. We were at war with Germany again and we were going to have to be real soldiers.

Chapter Two

Round Trip

They didn't give us long to brood about it. Within minutes we were paraded and mobilised. All the ceremonial kit, the bearskins, scarlet tunics, grey capes and greatcoats and the everyday service dress had to be handed in. Personal kit, civilian clothes and so on, had to be packed in suitcases and sent home. We were among the first units to be issued with the new battledress, and from now on it was to be battledress all the time, including steel helmet and respirator. I didn't know it then but for the next six years I was to spend most of my waking hours and a good many of my sleeping ones in battledress. Like thousands of other men I even got married in it.

We also had to hand in our beautifully polished rifles and bayonets, which we were very reluctant to part with after the hours of effort that had gone into them. They were replaced by new black, greasy rifles and shorter, black-coated bayonets that came with strict instructions that no part of them was to be polished. This took some getting used to after years of being told our rifles weren't shiny enough. Having cleaned off the grease we spent a long time on the rifle range zeroing them in with what seemed like unlimited supplies of ammunition. The King inspected us on 7 September and we drove to Southampton the next day. I was now part of 1 Guards Brigade, 1st Division, one of the few fully equipped Divisions the British Army had at the time.

We landed at Cherbourg and drove across France towards the Belgian border more or less ready to do our bit. We were billeted in towns and villages along the French side of the border and then nothing warlike happened for the next nine months. We spent most of the time either digging, playing cards or practising schoolboy French on the girls. It was a huge but not unwelcome anticlimax, and if this was war I felt I could suffer any amount of it.

For political reasons the Maginot Line, the massive French frontier defences facing Germany, came to a halt at the Belgian border. We were put to work to continue the defences through France to the coast by building the Gort Line, and this was straight out of the First World War textbook. Trench lines were paced out by the officers on reverse slopes, marked with white tape then dug out with pick and shovel. We dug strong points and pillboxes, dressing stations and rallying points. We felled trees to clear lines of fire and used the timber to reinforce steep-sided ditches to trap tanks. Looking back on it you can see we were thoroughly trained and superbly equipped to win the First World War. If we had fought the Battle of the Somme trained and equipped as we were in 1939 it really would have been all over by Christmas, no sweat. But the Germans, unsporting as ever, had changed the rules without telling us. We were twenty years behind the times and didn't know it yet.

My pal Hook and I with some of the others were taken off this work early on to help with the harvest. This was not a bad job, with lots of girls around aching for some young male company, and always a blowout meal with plenty of wine and cider at the end of the day. We often managed to make it back to our billets in time for the dinner they had been keeping warm for us there – we were growing lads.

My Battalion spent December 1939 manning a section of the Maginot Line. It was every bit as impressive as we had been told, four lines of defences-in-depth stretching back for miles from the frontier, including the spectacular underground fortresses we had all heard about. They were so formidable that they are still there sixty years later, too tough to demolish. The French Army gave us a guided tour of these huge concrete mazes but that was all we saw of them.

Our job was the one the French soldiers didn't want, especially not in December – to man the two lines of open trenches in front of the forts. So we manned the trenches, just like our Dads had done twenty years before, all ready to break up the massed infantry attacks the Germans were going to make, just like their Dads had done twenty years before. It snowed a lot and was freezing cold and I never once saw a German. We patrolled no man's land at night to check the barbed wire and listen for German activity. I suppose they were doing much the same from their side, but only for the sake of appearances. The Maginot Line was so strong that when the time came the German Army naturally did the sensible thing. They went round the end of it.

I was now platoon truck driver. As well as normal duties I made a daily trip back to the Battalion supply depot to load up with rations, water and ammunition. Tip was the second driver and Butch Baker, the first aid man, usually rode with us because he kept all his stores on the truck. We also carried the heavy equipment like digging tools, barbed wire, wiring stakes, Bren magazines and boxes of ammunition and grenades. The truck was equipped with a Bren gun to be mounted on a collapsible stand for use as an anti-aircraft weapon. Two problems here: neither Tip nor I had been trained as anti-aircraft gunners, while the stand was like a heavy-duty Meccano set that came in a box complete with a spanner and printed instructions. We just hoped that when they came the German aircraft would be slow enough to let us bolt it all together before they were in range. We also carried a Boys anti-tank rifle which came in very handy when things warmed up.

Not long after New Year 1940 I had two weeks leave and went home. I was a bit surprised to be treated like a returning hero when all I had done was dig holes, drive a truck and chat up girls, but I kept quiet. As long as the club members, most of them old soldiers, were buying me drinks, I was quite happy to be a returning hero. A month or so later, back in France, Mum sent me a birthday cake and Tip, Hooky and the others helped me celebrate my twenty-first birthday in the right style.

When the German advance began we followed our much publicised master plan and advanced boldly into Belgium to meet them as near to their own frontier as possible. Some of the Belgians were less than happy about this, lobbing rocks as we drove past, but you can't please everybody. The genuine as opposed to the phoney war began for me near Louvain, where once again there was a pacing out of trenches and a laying out of white tape and a dishing out of tools from the back of my truck.

The digging began all over again. As well as the digging, miles of barbed wire was being laid and I had to make several trips back for more, but try as I might I couldn't get out of all the work. The Company Sergeant Major begged me to give some practical assistance with a shovel between trips. He also insisted that every inch of the fifty-foot white tapes was scraped clean before they were rolled up and slung on the truck. Guess who got that job?

We were ready for them in a surprisingly short time. Again, like so many British armies throughout history, we were superbly trained to win the last war. Sensibly enough, Jerry left us strictly alone. As with the Maginot Line, why attack strength when you can blitz through weakness? Nothing happened for a day or two, then we began to fall back, the first backward step along a very confusing road. Nobody knew why we were falling back, or if they did they weren't telling me. Jerry hadn't come anywhere near us, not even from the air, but working to our Great War ideas we had to fall back to keep in touch with our flanks and preserve the line.

The supply system was still operating, although my daily trips back to the depot were taking longer and longer. The more we fell back the more difficult it became to move at all because the roads were clogged with civilians. Some were driving cars or trucks or horses and carts, but most were on foot pushing barrows, prams or bikes. They were all loaded with furniture and bedding and they were all desperate to get away from the invading Germans. As far as falling back was concerned, our troops could easily march across the fields, but driving the truck I had to use the roads. We couldn't move faster than a crawl at the best of times and I began to wonder whether being platoon truck driver was such a good idea after all.

Life began to get difficult. We would set out at dawn with lists of the rations and ammunition the platoon needed. The first problem was to find the supply depot, which was never in the same place twice because they were busy falling back as well. When we did find it we grabbed whatever we could lay hands on and drove back to look for the platoon, which by this time had also moved somewhere else. We were usually lucky to find them before dark, and then there would be hell to pay from the CSM because we were late.

We baled out of the truck several times when German aircraft attacked the road. Our hopes of using our anti-aircraft Bren disappeared, as Jerry always came in very fast and very low and we were always too busy diving for the ditch to put that stand together. One evening Tip spent an hour building it in the back of the truck so that with part of the canvas top rolled up we could have a go back. I cannot remember whether we ever did, but it's the thought that counts. Bombs might hit the road or land alongside it, or the aircraft would make a strafing run with machine guns. We did what we could for the wounded then I drove on while Tip and Butch walked ahead shoving broken carts and dead horses out of the way. We felt lousy doing it, but we had a platoon to feed.

I remember lying nose to nose with an old bloke in a ditch while the crap flew around above us. When the Jerries had gone he looked at me and said, 'Blimey! You British?' We got talking and it turned out that he had deserted from our army during the First World War, settled down with a local widow and lived in that part of France ever since. He said some very rude things about Germans then shambled off to find his widow and his horse and cart.

Things got serious as we were squeezed closer to the coast. I remember another occasion when the First World War came back to haunt us. We had been ordered to dislodge some Germans who had crossed a canal and were shooting at us across a field. Our Lieutenant was telling the Sergeant how this was to be done; the Sergeant was clearly not happy but couldn't say so. We were sheltering behind an earth bank which had a gap in it but no gate. We were to fix bayonets, the Lieutenant said, and follow him through the gap. Once through we were to spread out left and right, form into a line and advance on the canal bank to clear it of the enemy. The Lieutenant then drew his revolver, flicked the safety catch and walked – walked, mind you – through the gap. We followed him, of course, running fit to bust and crouching low. I ran twenty yards into the field past him, stone dead, revolver still in hand. We shifted the Jerries, but what a waste. And I cannot even remember his name.

Beside yet another canal Tip and I had our one chance to use the Boys rifle. This weapon was another legacy from the First World War, during which it might well have been a vital piece of kit, but it was now sadly outclassed. It was simply a very heavy rifle, in every sense of the word. It weighed a ton and fired a massive hardened steel slug that would punch its way through tank armour to do nasty things to the men inside – if the armour was thin enough. Other people elsewhere in this battle were finding out that the Jerries had already thought of that one. The weapon needed two men to use it, one to aim and fire, the other to lay across his legs to cope with the recoil. Tip and I had been lugging the thing and its ammunition around for hours as well as our own rifles, and I was determined to do something with it even if it was only to drop it in the nearest shell hole.

Once again Jerry had the near bank of the canal and was keeping our heads down with a machine gun. We were waiting for artillery support but nothing much was happening; like everything else, communications were a mess. Then I had my brain wave, suggesting to our Corporal that I could put a few anti-tank rounds through the canal bank where the machine gun was firing. The rounds were supposed to be armour piercing so surely they would go through a few feet of earth. He passed the idea on, no doubt taking credit for it as he did so, and it eventually reached an officer who gave permission to fire. Tip and I sorted ourselves out and I put five rounds through the bank, aiming about two feet below the top. The machine gun stopped firing for a few minutes then started up again, so I fired twice more. No more machine gun fire and I'm the blushing hero, then the order came to fall back and we were off, still carrying the Boys rifle between us. I have often wondered what the Jerries made of those great slugs tearing through the canal bank. They obviously did someone no good at all.

Soon after this I was wounded. Apart from a broken finger later on in the desert this was the only wound I had during the entire war, so wasn't I the lucky one?

After hours of searching we had found the supply depot along a side road behind a school. The usual crowds of civvies were shuffling along the high road watching the sky. Butch was sorting and loading his first aid stuff into the cab, Tip was chucking boxes up to me and I was stacking them in the back of the truck, when we heard a plane. From where I was standing I could see over the playground wall, and a Jerry was flying towards us along the road. By now this was really all they had to do, there was no need to waste ammunition because the civvies were leaping for the ditch and scattering into the fields just at the sound of his engines, but this particular Jerry dropped a stick of bombs. I stood there fascinated, watching them sail down, and they started exploding as I ducked. One of them went off somewhere behind me, slamming me into the wall.

I woke up feeling dizzy and thick-headed. Tip had dragged me under the truck and Butch was working on my left foot, which didn't hurt but was twisted over at an incredible angle. Lumps of shrapnel were sticking out of my knees as well, and Butch was splinting and bandaging and telling me everything would be all right, they'd get me to a dressing station pronto. Now, I didn't like the sound of that. I knew we were leaving wounded men behind for the Germans to capture and I am told I made a fuss. Since it was my funeral they shrugged, finished loading, lifted me into the truck and set off to find the platoon. I spent the next six days in the back of that truck, dozing and waking without really knowing where I was. That didn't matter because no one else knew where they were either. I suppose I was concussed. Most of my waking time passed charging Bren magazines and priming hand grenades and giving them out to anyone who wanted them. Our men were using ammunition as fast as Tip could deliver it so it must have helped a bit to have it ready for instant use.

We came across the Battalion doctor in a bone yard next to an abattoir. He was worked to death but Butch talked him into coming to have a look at my ankle. Only then did I realize that Butch had been pumping me full of something to stop the pain, bless him, which is why it didn't hurt and why I kept going to sleep. The doctor took the shrapnel out of my legs then got Butch and Tip to sit on me while he pulled the ankle joint back in. It still didn't hurt until he stuck a needle in my backside, which did, and told me to go to sleep. I have never needed to be told that twice but that bone yard stank and was full of rats making little scrabbly noises. I suppose I was coming down from the drugs Butch had been giving me for the best part of a week and I was wide awake all night, but at least Jerry left us alone.

Tip was finally ordered to make for Le Panne on the Belgian coast north of Dunkirk. The Battalion had been drawn into the perimeter defence of the port and we finally began to twig what was going on. MPs stopped us on the outskirts and made Tip drive into a field, where he had to disable the truck by draining the sump and running the engine till it seized. Ammunition had to be off-loaded and that is when the MPs found me. Butch and Tip were ordered to take me to the dressing station in the sand dunes then rejoin the platoon, and they said, 'Yes, Sergeant' like the good boys they were. Once out of earshot they changed their tune. 'We're not leaving you, mate,' Butch said, 'you could be our ticket home!'

I think we were there for three days but I was back on drugs and cannot be sure. I know we didn't eat much. I lay there watching the long lines of men and the ships coming in to the rickety pier to take them off. Air attacks seemed to be going on all the time, the explosions of bombs, or maybe shells, were constant.

A white-painted hospital ship plastered with red crosses came alongside the pier. The stretcher bearers and Red Cross orderlies told me there was a chance they could get me on it but they would take all the seriously wounded first. A couple of hours later the hospital ship began to back out. No room for me, then, but as the ship slowly backed away from the jetty a flock of dive bombers appeared and bombed it, screaming down one after another. I lay on the sand and watched the hits and the clouds of smoke until the ship settled on the bottom with just the tips of her masts and the tops of her funnels to be seen. 'Never mind, mate,' Tip said, nudging me, 'there'll be another one along tomorrow!'

It might have been next morning when Butch and Tip came to tell me that the Guards were being concentrated about two miles down the beach. The remaining men of our Battalion were being taken out on the next boat, the two of them had been ordered to go and they offered to help me down there. Or, they said, if I wanted I could stay here and wait for the next hospital ship. After my grandstand view of what happened to the last hospital ship, I went with them. When we arrived there was none other than RSM Hector Young, who had been my training Sergeant Major at Caterham, busily organising everything in sight. He had little time for us.

'Where's your helmet, Feebery?'

'Lost it, sir!'

'And where's your rifle? Lost that too I suppose? Wait here!' He stalked off in disgust and came back pulling open the sling of a rifle which he hung round my neck before plonking a steel helmet on my head. 'Right! Now you are properly dressed! What about ammunition?'

'Bloody hell, sir!' Tip pipes up, 'he's heavy enough already!', and the RSM, bless his heart, grinned at him and told us all to go forth and multiply.

We joined the line of men and stood there while it got dark. A destroyer came alongside and we shuffled forward on to the wooden jetty which was about 200 yards long. This was the dodgy bit because Jerry was still bombing and strafing and men were diving for cover. The destroyer's guns were firing and the three of us just kept moving forward – there was nothing else we could do. When we got within shouting distance Tip bellowed, 'Wounded man here!' loud enough to be heard over the racket, and the crowd in front parted to let us through. A couple of matelots grabbed me and passed me forward while Tip and Butch were sent aft. I have never met either of them since.

I was helped to a stretcher and strapped in so tight I couldn't move. It was then upended and passed down through narrow hatches in three decks until I was laid out alongside dozens of other men somewhere deep inside the ship. All I could think about was that hospital ship slowly settling on the bottom – how many men on board her had been strapped into stretchers? – but there was nothing I could do about it. I lay there listening to the ship's gunfire and the heavy thumps of bombs going off until a civilian doctor arrived and gave me an injection.

I knew nothing more until I woke up on deck in Dover harbour. They laid us out on a big pallet, eight at a time, and swayed us off the deck with a dockside crane. We were carried into a hospital train and after a long wait it started moving. Nurses kept coming through with cups of tea and as many fags as you could smoke, while the train stopped and started and stood in stations for what seemed like hours. Everybody was guessing where we were going. All the station names had been removed to confound the enemy when they invaded; it worked even better on us, we were totally confounded. At every stop some men would be taken off. I can remember the train rolling very slowly through Norwood Junction station and telling anyone who would listen that this would do me, I could crawl home from here! It fell dark again as we rolled through London and out the other side, heading north as far as we could tell.

I woke up to find the sun streaming through the windows as they carried me off the train at Sheffield Victoria station. Next thing I knew I was in Wharncliffe Hospital, where a very brisk nurse told me her name was Connie as she set about giving me a blanket bath. We got chatting, as you do when a young woman is stripping you naked, and a bit later her younger sister turned up dishing out fags and fruit along the ward. That was the first I saw of Vera, my wife.

I later had something of a fit. In my respirator case, which I had looked after very carefully all the way to Le

Panne and on to that destroyer, I had the accumulated winnings of nearly ten months dedicated pontoon playing, about twenty pounds. I know it was there when I went aboard the destroyer but it wasn't there now. I just hope whoever took it ended up with the hangover he deserved.

Another way of looking at it is that only one hundred and eighty men of the 3rd Battalion Grenadier Guards were taken off the beaches around Dunkirk out of over a thousand who'd landed at Cherbourg the year before. From that point of view twenty quid seems a very reasonable price to pay.

Chapter Three

Commando

I was in Wharnecliffe Hospital for about two weeks. Dobby Dobson, another pal from my Company, and I could soon get out and about on crutches. We hobbled home for tea and buns with Connie and Vera a few times and were getting on very nicely thank you when we were told to get ready to move. Ten minutes later I was on a train to Harrogate and ended up in St Ethelburga's Girls School where I convalesced.

It couldn't last for ever. I was examined and classified B2, fit for light duties, and went back to Wellington Barracks Holding Battalion in London. There my 'light duties' consisted of the wonderful job of Company Sergeant Major's batman, the army word for a servant. It was as if the last twelve months had never happened. Hundreds of men I had known for years were either dead or prisoners. While I shined the CSM's buttons and polished his boots and ironed his shirts, as well as my own, I knew very well that but for a couple of good pals I might now be doing exactly the same job in a prison camp. I couldn't really grumble. If nothing else I was learning to count my blessings even while I wondered how I was going to get out of this mess and back into the war.

Then one of my very best pals turned up. John Bowers had been badly wounded at Dunkirk and lay in hospital in London for weeks. He was held together by stitches but just about fit enough to get around without crutches if he took it easy. He reported to the barracks daily while convalescing and we happened to meet. This was too good to miss so I wangled myself an evening pass and we hit the town. We must have had a drink or two because some time later, and long, long after we should both have been back indoors, we were sitting on the kerb somewhere in Holborn, just sitting there, sharing a bottle of something, nice and peaceful, yarning about old times and old friends as you do when you are in that state.

Then this copper loomed over us. 'What d'you think you two are doing, then?' says Old Bill.

We explained that we were wounded soldiers, shooting him the same line that had worked like a charm in every pub we had been to. It certainly accounted for the state we were in. The copper took a different view.

'Oh yes?' he said, all superior. 'A couple of Dunkirk runners, are we?'

We saw red at that and flattened him. Some of his pals heard the noise and joined in. Half an hour and several badly damaged policemen later, we were banged up in Holborn nick with John bleeding buckets from the wounds in his back and legs that had barely healed. He had really been through hell, and the coppers were embarrassed but tried hard not to show it. The ambulance people had to stitch him up there and then in the cell before they could even take him back to hospital. I was suddenly sober enough to explain myself to the MPs they had called and was carted back to Wellington Barracks where the orderly officer told me my fortune in painful detail. It was quite a night.

My salvation came in the form of a notice on the Company notice board. They were looking for volunteers from men returning to the Holding Battalion and from young soldiers who had just finished their training to form a 'special unit'. They particularly wanted men who could drive, swim and ride a bike or a horse – just up my alley, so I put my name down. A few days later I was summoned before the Commanding Officer, who went through the details on the notice.

'How many of these things can you do, Feebery?'

'I can drive, swim and ride a bike, sir.'

'I see. Are you fit?'

'Graded B1, sir.'

'Very well. See the Medical Officer this afternoon. If he gives you A1 I'll consider you as a possible candidate.'

My injuries had healed and there was nothing showing from the dislocated ankle. The doctor was happy to grade me A1 and pass the news on to the CO, and two days later I was summoned for the last time. Four other men had been accepted as well and the CO gave us some more details. We would be paid six shillings and nine pence a day (a small fortune for a Private), allowed to wear civilian clothes and be billeted in civilian houses during training. If we still fancied the idea we were to report at the Guard Room at seven next morning, kit packed and ready to move.

Came the dawn, and to our surprise we were invited to climb into a large and very comfortable staff car. The driver told us we could smoke, so we lit up and asked him what this was all about. He told us he had been collecting groups of men like us every morning for the last two weeks and taking them to Burnham-on-Crouch, out along the Thames estuary in Essex, but apart from that he was none the wiser. All we could do was sit back and enjoy the ride, so we did. Later that day we found we'd joined 4 Independent Company, Grenadier Guards.

Needless to say we never were paid six and nine a day nor did we ever wear civvy clothes, but we were billeted out in pairs. My partner was Fred Crookes and our landlady mothered us. We both left our fifteen shillings boarding money on the mantelpiece every Friday but she wouldn't touch it. By the Tuesday we were broke, of course, and she would tell us to take the cash away, it was cluttering up her mantel. We paraded every day and trained mostly by route marching from Burnham to Steeple and back. They sent us rowing on the river once or twice and it was nice while it lasted, but it didn't last long. There were fifty or more men kicking around Burnham when they shifted us all to Inverary on Loch Fyne in Scotland, and somewhere during that long, long train ride I became a member of 2 Troop, 8 Commando, who were all Grenadier Guards.

Commando training can best be described as *intensive*. Our days were spent going up the mountain and down the mountain, then up the mountain and down the mountain again. There was field craft training, map and compass reading, night marching, unarmed combat, weapons training with pistols and light automatics, then up the bloody mountain yet again. There were a few huts but we ordinary soldiers and most of the NCOs and officers lived in two-man tents. The only water was what splashed and trickled past in the burns around the camp. Shaving was a daily ordeal, and I still cannot stomach porridge.

One of the few things I can clearly remember about this time is the CO's passion for socks. Every man was ordered to parade with a dry pair of socks, to be presented for inspection on demand. This was not an easy order to obey because it rained most of the time, but woe betide the man whose dry socks turned out to be even slightly damp. Take it from me there are far worse ways to pass a wet and windy night in Scotland than lying in your blankets in your tent listening to the rain hissing down outside while drying a sock over a candle ready for next morning's parade.

Chapter Four

Foreign Parts

Brigadier General Laycock was ordered to form a Middle East Commando to carry out operations against targets in the Mediterranean. Numbers 7, 8 and 11 Commando were selected for the job and were known collectively as 'Layforce'. Layforce sailed from Gourock in January 1941 on the passenger liners SS *Glenroy,* SS *Glenearn* and SS *Glengyle* that had been specially fitted out as Commando landing ships. Among other adaptations they carried landing craft on their lifeboat davits. Our convoy called at Freetown, Sierra Leone, and Cape Town where we were allowed ashore and were met on the dockside by a crowd of South Africans inviting us to their homes. A few of us were taken away by an Afrikaner who was a high official in the railways. He had a beautiful house half way up a mountain where we had a slap-up meal and more than enough to drink. He drove us round to see the sights, finishing on top of Table Mountain itself. It was a really wonderful day after being cooped up on a ship for a fortnight. The convoy carried on round Africa, ducking into Durban because of submarines, then up through the Red Sea to Egypt and along the Suez Canal to the Bitter Lakes, where we disembarked and set up our base depot at Naharia.

Then it was back to good old training again, but at least there weren't any mountains and it wasn't raining. We were in Guards' tropical kit by now, short-sleeved shirts, baggy shorts below the knee and heavy white pith helmets to keep the sun from our dainty brows. The next couple of months were very frustrating. Operations were planned and cancelled one after another. I have read about the reasons for this since, but at the time we just seemed to be hanging around doing no good to anyone. Thundering battles were going on all around us, in Abyssinia to the south, in the Libyan desert to the west and in Greece and Yugoslavia across the Mediterranean to the north, and we just stayed there, training. You cannot keep hundreds of extremely fit and aggressive young men sitting around doing nothing, and there were some spectacular tear-ups between the three Commandos.

There were some efforts to make use of us. I was detailed as a member of a special raiding force and went aboard HMS *Gnat*, a flat-bottomed, shallow-draft river gunboat, originally designed for service in China and the Far East. The idea now was that she and her sister ship HMS *Firefly* would creep along the coast to bombard Tobruk, then occupied by the Italians. Both ships were fitted with two huge guns, one at each end, that seemed enormous and completely out of proportion to the size of the ships. There was no accommodation so we made ourselves comfortable on deck, trying to keep out of the way of the matelots. As soon as we left Alexandria harbour the ships began to pitch and roll and most of us were seasick.

Near Tobruk we were told to stand to because the bombardment was about to begin, and we mustered tight together amidships and waited. We were still trying to work out why they needed such a large number of soldiers on board when no landing was planned. It then began to dawn on us that those dirty great guns were fixed, and to aim a gun they had to turn the whole ship until it was pointing in the right direction. A shouted warning was followed by **CRUMP** as one of the guns fired. The bows went down, the stern came up and we all got soaked while clinging on for dear life. Then the ship slowly turned round until the other gun was aimed, then **CRUMP** again with the same result. We then dipped and heaved all the way back to Alexandria, having realized that we were only on board as extra ballast to keep the tub afloat in the open sea. The air raid warning sounded as we entered the harbour. A tiny black dot appeared high in the sky and we were given permission to fire. By this time we were ready to demolish anything Italian and let loose with every weapon we had, even pistols and Tommy guns, in the general direction of the aircraft. A bomb burst in the sea about a mile away while the black dot fled into the haze whence it came.

The delays and cancellations to our Commando operations were caused by the efforts being made to evacuate our forces from Greece and Crete. Our three converted liners had been sent to help with the evacuations soon after we arrived and we never saw them or their specialised equipment again. We tried landing from destroyers, working from HMS *Decoy*, but it wasn't really on. It was difficult getting large numbers of men on and off the ship and we could never get close enough to the beach. It was finally decided there was nothing we could usefully do as Commandos in the Middle East, and many of the men were simply returned to their 'parent' units if they were in the region, while the rest of us were sent to Naharia depot to await transport home. I had recently been made Corporal for the third time and had the great honour of being appointed permanent Orderly Corporal for the ex-Commandos.

Office work. Pencil pushing and paper shuffling. Running errands for the Orderly Officer. Making tea. Taking the blame for everything from running out of carbon paper to not emptying the waste paper baskets. All in the heat of the Egyptian desert. This, I thought, is my shining future in the Grenadier Guards. We were sitting around waiting for orders and tempers flared easily. One job I had was to escort four men to the Geneifa Field Punishment Centre. They were all friends of mine, as were my armed escort of three more Grenadiers. I reported to the Regimental Sergeant Major at Headquarters to collect my prisoners and the travel warrants.

The RSM was Biff McCall, a great soldier who learned his business before the First World War and must have been fifty when I knew him. He passed over the bumf and said, 'Feebery, I give you ten to one in shillings you don't get 'em past Cairo!'

'You're on, sir!' I said, but I never did collect. Days later he was taken out of active service because of his age and given a desk job behind the lines. I believe he took to drink and the last I heard he had been reduced to Corporal, poor old sod.

My happy band of pilgrims was driven to the station in Alexandria where I reported to the Rail Transport Officer and got them on board. Shortly after we set off Bob Bennett said, 'Here, Fee, how about taking these flaming handcuffs off?'

'OK,' I said, doing my Humphrey Bogart tough guy impression, 'but they go back on before we get to Cairo, and if anybody tries to leg it I will personally attend to him!'

It sounded good, but the train from Alex to Cairo crawls across empty desert at walking pace with lots of stops and starts. Old Biff knew what he was talking about when he made that bet. If it had been me going to Geneifa and knowing what I was in for when I got there, I might well have chanced it and done a runner, but those four men were as good as gold all the way. The cuffs went back on as we entered Cairo, where there was an MP truck waiting to take us to cells and barracks for an overnight stay. I delivered my prisoners and went back to Naharia and the filing and the rubber stamps. I did learn to use a typewriter there so it wasn't time completely wasted. It just felt as though it was.

One evening John Riley, Andy Seddon and I went into Alexandria for a drink and met up with George Barnes, another Grenadier we knew from 8 Commando. He was a reservist called back to the colours from his civvy job as a lifeguard and swimming instructor on Blackpool beach. I believe he ended up as an officer somewhere in the Far East, but on this evening he spent most of the time telling the three of us about the work he was doing in the Folboat Section, and this office boy listened with envy. We had heard about Folboats in Scotland but never had anything to do with them. They were two-seater canoes that could be dismantled and stored in a couple of kit bags when not in use. I found out long after the war that they were actually a German idea.

Folboat Section men were trained to use these canoes to go ashore secretly ahead of a Commando raid, survey the beach for obstacles and opposition and mark out the landing area for the main force. They had developed this to a fine art in Scotland under Captain Roger Courtney, a famous pre-war explorer who, among many other feats, had once canoed the length of the River Nile. When Layforce was disbanded he had managed to keep his small band of specialists in being by offering their services to the Navy, and George and his pals were now based in the submarine depot ship HMS *Medway* moored in Alexandria harbour. They were training to go out in the boats of the First Submarine Flotilla, that was based on *Medway*, to make Commando-style raids on enemy coasts.

Now this sounded a bit more like it, and a lot more attractive than being Orderly Corporal. When George dropped the hint that they were looking for a few more volunteers, Andy, John and I looked at each other and grinned. We chewed over the fine points with George and put in a request for transfer next day. Our Adjutant could not quite understand why anyone would want to give up real soldiering to join a Mickey Mouse outfit like the Folboat Section, but after a lot of heart searching and head shaking he approved the request. We were told to report to Captain Courtney as soon as possible.

That looked like being easier said than done. None of the sentries on the dock in Alexandria knew what we were on about. We were showing them our chits yet again when a boat came alongside and a few men got out. The coxswain overheard us as he lit a fag. 'Are you Folboat Section?' he shouted up. We agreed that we'd like to be if we could ever find it. 'C'mon,' he said, 'I'll give you a lift', and he ferried us out to the *Medway*.

Roger Courtney was a short, stocky man, all muscle. He looked us over, asked a few questions about our service and so on and seemed satisfied. He said he would take us on probation for a few weeks, we could make a start on the basic training and if we suited, we were in. If not, it was back to Naharia and that bloody office.

We were sent to HMS *Saunders*, a combined operations centre run by the Navy on the shores of the Great Bitter Lake at Kabrit. We had our own camp within the base but messed with the Navy. There were about a dozen of us all told and we spent most of the time swimming very long distances and learning to use Folboats, inflatable dinghies and six-oared Navy cutters. They also introduced us to specialised weapons like the limpet mines used to attack moored ships. The instructors cheerfully admitted that nobody really knew what we might be called upon to do. They worked on the assumption that, once ashore, we should be ready to do just about anything from sabotage to treating wounds to staying alive on the run if things went wrong. I think I am right in saying the we were the last Folboat section men to be 'trained' to use the submarine escape apparatus, which shows just how make-it-up-as-you-go-along the whole thing was. This is something submariners have to learn, of course, and it was taken for granted that we ought to know the drill as well. The trouble was there were no proper facilities or training tanks nearer than Portsmouth.

John, Andy and I spent a very pleasant afternoon with a couple of Petty Officers who showed us how to put on the breathing apparatus and explained the routine. When it came to actually practising an escape we strolled out to the end of a jetty where a couple of old dustbins had been welded end to end and dunked in the water. They were meant to simulate the escape chamber of a submarine. One by one we solemnly strapped lead weights to our boots, dropped off the jetty and wandered around on the lake bed for a bit getting used to the breathing sets, then popped up through the welded dustbins to the surface for a smoke while we dried off in the sun. The two matelots were killing themselves laughing. As one of them told us, 'If it ever comes to it you lot won't be the first out! Just watch the others, you'll soon get the hang of it!'

A real submarine was provided for training in the Red Sea but it was not exactly a front-line boat. HMS *Papanikolous* had been sailed away from Greece by her Captain and crew when the Germans invaded, and on arrival in Alexandria she had been adopted into the Royal Navy for the duration. The boat carried one British officer and a British wireless operator but the rest of the crew were the Greek sailors who had pinched her in the first place. They were great lads to work with and it did not matter that nobody could understand anybody else.

They took us out for a dive to show us how the boat worked, which was all very interesting until we hit the bottom hard and stuck. I think there might have been a bit of showing off on the part of the Greek matelots, who were very proud of their boat. However it happened, we sat there for a while with the British officer explaining what was being done to unstick us with a confidence I don't think he really felt, until after some time the boat pulled free and made for the surface, going up like a lift then leaping from the water and smacking down again with a thump that made our teeth rattle. Somewhat subdued we went ashore and made for the NAAFI, more than ready for a few beers.

This was when the real training began and when the

practical problems came to light. We practised assembling and launching Folboats from the submarine's casing at night, which was fairly easy because we could already put them together blindfold. Paddling ashore to a precise spot and landing there in silence came with experience. The hardest bit by far was finding the submarine again when we paddled back out to sea. We never did solve this problem either in training or during the real thing. You had to make allowance for currents drifting the sub away from where she was supposed to be while also making allowance for those same currents on the Folboat. Then there was the wind. Inflatable dinghies skid about like bubbles in the lightest breeze even with four large men aboard paddling fit to bust. There was nothing much the matelots could do to help us. If a surfaced submarine showed a light or made too much noise off an enemy coast it would become an instant and very tasty target. All they could do was take the risk of staying on the surface, patrol exactly on rendezvous and be patient.

Our training cruise over we went back to Tewfik and tied up. We were waiting for a truck to take us to Kabrit and beds that didn't rock, just lying about sunbathing on the submarine casing, when somebody shouted, 'Look out! Sharks!' We took no notice, it was only one of the Greek lads trying it on, when there was a swish alongside and a ten-foot shark swept past our dangling legs. It was the fastest I ever saw the Folboat Section move. On the dockside somebody told us that sharks were quite common in the Red Sea and often came scrounging for food among the gash ditched overboard in the harbour. We thought of the happy hours we'd just spent swimming around and falling out of Folboats in the dark and finished our sunbathing on the quay.

Trained as well as anybody could tell we moved back to HMS *Medway* and set up our mess on board. All dressed up with nowhere to go, for a few days we went fishing off the rocks in the outer harbour and had a run ashore most nights. The Navy made us honorary members of the Fleet Club so there was always somewhere to go for a drink or a game of bingo. They sometimes had boxing nights when all comers could climb in the ring with a Navy pro and earn a pound a round plus a fiver for a knockout. One evening I was skint and very thirsty and decided to have a go. They asked my weight and whether I had boxed before, and when I told them only as an amateur they agreed to let me keep my vest on for the sake of appearances. There were no size twelve slippers so I climbed into the ring in my socks.

My second, another matelot, was busy telling me what a great boxer the other bloke was when the referee started talking to the crowd. I caught something about the eight-round clash of two top-ranking heavyweights that was about to take place before their very eyes and nearly climbed out, but bets were changing hands and I was stony broke so I stood up and stayed out of trouble for the eight rounds. The other bloke was good and I was only too happy with a draw. I was happier still with the eight quid and the beers it bought me.

The Folboat section was now about twenty strong. A suitable target for a raid would be identified and two of us would be briefed to go aboard a regular submarine patrol and raid it. It was clearly understood that submarine operations came first and our jobs were very much a secondary affair – every landing was at the skipper's discretion, depending entirely on whether he had the time and opportunity to land us and pick us up again. After a while and a bit of experience two of us went to sea with every sortie whether or not a job had been set up first. That way, if the skipper saw a chance to do some damage, or if base found a target that could be wirelessed through to the sub, we were on the spot ready to go and do it. It wasn't long before we Folboat section men had put in more time underwater than some of the matelots, and we didn't let them forget it.

Chapter Five

Underwater Grenadiers

There was only one occasion to my knowledge when the Folboat Section did the job it had been created to do – to recce the landing beach for a Commando raid. This was Operation Flipper, the so-called Rommel Raid, and what a mess it was.

The plan was to land a force of Commandos from the sea behind enemy lines who would attempt to kill or capture the German General Rommel at his headquarters, said to be located some distance inland at Beda Littoria. What we did not know then, of course, was that the whole thing was based on faulty intelligence. Rommel was not even in Africa at the time of the raid and the place had never been his headquarters. So much for intelligence, but we did not know that then.

Most of the Folboat Section and sixty Commandos under the command of Colonel Geoffrey Keyes were crammed into two submarines, HMS *Torbay* and HMS *Talisman*. They surfaced off the Libyan coast during the night of 17 November 1941 and two Folboat teams went away to do their job ashore. The rest of the Folboat Section, including me, were detailed to inflate dinghies on the submarine casings and get the Commandos and their gear safely to the beach. It was a filthy night with a strong wind and a heavy sea slopping spray all over the casing and making it really slippery. The dinghies had to be inflated with a hand pump like a large version of what anyone else would use on a bike tyre, and once they had been inflated the wind was blowing them straight off the boat. Some of the men slipped in as well but we got them back safe and sound.

When the shore party signalled 'all clear' the fun really began as we started to take the men to the beach. With the wind blowing directly on shore and everybody in the dinghy paddling like fury we made it through the surf. It was much easier to tow a dinghy than paddle it into that wind, so I swam back to the sub towing the empties to be deflated and stowed. The subs had been surfaced for three hours before the Commandos were all on their way. I was shattered, but those men were just as wet and tired as I was and still had a long night's march in front of them before they could rest. At least I could get below in the warm and dry off properly.

The plan was for *Torbay* to come back four days later to take them off from the same beach. Some cheerful soul of a staff officer had obviously decided that one submarine would be enough, allowing for casualties. Meanwhile the boat made a patrol along the coast.

The skipper of *Torbay* was Lieutenant Commander Anthony 'Gamp' Miers, and I had a lot to do with this officer. He was a pugnacious individual who rubbed a lot of people up the wrong way, but we usually got on all right. I think that was because I talked to him in the same language he used to me, stripes or no stripes. Once when he was a bit excited he said, 'What would you do if I punched you on the nose, Feebery?' He was solidly built but not my size at all. 'I would probably punch you back, sir,' I said, hoping he wouldn't. He laughed and it all passed off, but he was always pushing people that way.

After we had landed the Commandos we sat on the bottom until dusk the next day, when Gamp announced that he wanted to do something to distract the enemy and it was about time the gun's crew had some exercise. There were no passengers on Gamp's boat and he had told the Folboat Section right from the start that there would be work for us to do under way even though we were only brown jobs. Because I was a big strong lad he had made me second lift on the ammunition supply during a gun action. The shells for the deck gun were stored deep in the guts of the boat and a sailor went down there to pass them up to me one by one. I had to lift them up through a hatch to another sailor, who passed them out to the gun's crew on the casing.

There was a Jerry airfield not far along the coast from the landing beach, at extreme range for our four-inch gun, but a few shells out of the blue might stir them up a bit. We came close inshore again, submerged until Gamp got his bearings and was fairly sure the coast was clear. We were all ready for a gun action except that the gun's crew were not on deck yet. I was cradling a shell ready to pass it up when the time came.

Then we surfaced. The sea was still very choppy and once the boat surfaced she began bouncing around all over the place. It is very difficult to keep your balance and heft a heavy shell through a small hole in the ceiling without touching the sides, but even so twenty rounds were fired and something was seen to be burning in the distance far inland. Nothing came our way at all.

We were back off the landing beach at the appointed time. The risk was taken of showing a light and signals came back, so some of the Commandos had survived the raid. The trouble was the weather had not changed, the gale was still blowing hard and it was another filthy night with an even heavier sea. Gamp decided it was too dangerous to try to get them off and once again risked a signal to say he would come back tomorrow. This was nothing out of the ordinary and we spent the day sitting on the bottom until it got dark. The weather did not seem so bad the following night and signals were being flashed out to sea, but they were not the ones we were expecting. Before he risked his boat on the surface again for any length of time Gamp wanted to be sure who was making them, so Lieutenant Tommy Langton and I went ashore in a Folboat to see what we could see.

The surf was enormous. We capsized on the way in but came ashore intact, then carried the Folboat across the open beach into cover among the undergrowth further up. Leaving it upside down with the paddles underneath where we could find it again we had a quiet walk round. We covered at least 500 yards in each direction along that beach, moving inland among the trees and bushes as carefully as we could.

There was nothing much to hear, what with the gale blowing and the trees thrashing about, but we both smelt a very large rat. Something was definitely not right. Once a cigarette glowed briefly. Bushes waggled in the wrong direction to the wind. Somebody was lurking around there for sure but whoever it was they had us spotted and were keeping right out of our way. If they had been our men surely they would have made contact. Enough was enough. Tommy beckoned, and we got back to the Folboat sharpish.

With the surf crashing onto the beach it was almost impossible to launch the canoe. We tried half a dozen times and in one wave Tommy lost his paddle. We both knew that the men playing hide and seek up in the bushes must be either Italians or Germans. Either way, we were likely to be nabbed any second, but even so we crawled along the edge of the surf for a while on hands and knees hunting for the paddle. I had the nasty feeling all the time that someone up there in the trees was staring at my back through the sights of his rifle.

Before long Tommy said, in effect, stuff this, let's go home. We finally managed to launch the Folboat and climb aboard. It had been holed during one of our many attempts to get seaborne so Tommy baled out the water while I paddled. We eventually found the sub more or less where we expected it and Tommy's report to Gamp boiled down to two words: forget it. The whole thing was a washout.

We found out much later that the Jerries had captured the men we had seen signalling the first night and then stayed there hoping to catch the sub on the surface. That's why they had left me and Tommy alone, they were after the boat not a couple of mermaids.

This incident also changed our procedures. We had been careful to make sure our weapons and explosives would survive a capsize (the Tommy gun and spare magazines were always lashed up in a lifejacket, for example) but the one thing a canoeist cannot afford to lose is his paddle. After this, every man secured his paddle to his wrist with a length of line before he stepped into the boat. Simple and obvious, perhaps, but we were learning all the time.

The Rommel Raid was a good job to walk away from. I believe I am right in saying that all but two of the men we put ashore were either killed or captured, and one of the survivors was Sergeant Jack Terry, a man I had known in the Grenadiers and 8 Commando.

Jock Booth and I were aboard *Torbay* when Gamp Miers won the Victoria Cross. That was a trip never to be forgotten even though all Jock and I did was take up space. The submarines of those days used powerful diesel engines to get around on the surface, and when the sea was calm they could move at a fair lick. The diesels doubled as generators to charge the batteries that powered the electric motors the boat relied on when submerged. Once under water, submarines were very slow and always seemed to me to creep around at a snail's pace, but they were also suprisingly quiet and peaceful. The electric motors made hardly any noise and any talking or passing of orders was usually pitched low. There's no need to raise your voice, unless you are being depth charged.

Gamp Miers' attitude to 'passengers' was understandable. There is no such thing as spare room in a submarine at any time and every man aboard has to be an expert in his job. Such skills as the Folboat Section possessed were useless when the boat was submerged; we were just ballast that breathed. For normal cruising stations Jock went forward to the torpedo room and I went aft to the engine room to balance things up. We were told to keep out of the way so I usually passed the time playing cards with the matelots. In action we had to stand one at each end of the control room and, you've guessed it, keep out of the way. At least we had some idea of what was going on outside, which is more than most of the matelots ever did.

On this particular trip we had been at sea for a few days, surfacing at night to run on the diesels and recharge the batteries. A lot of the matelots had a crafty smoke during the day even though smoking was totally banned when submerged. You could not smell it over all the other horrible smells, but their crimes came to light whenever we surfaced and opened the main hatch in the conning tower. It acted like a chimney, drawing up a cloud of tobacco smoke from both ends of the boat, and Gamp always went bananas. 'The bastards have been smoking again!' he would scream, climbing the wall, 'flogging's too good for 'em!' At least Jock and I had the chance to get some fresh air because one of our 'submariner' jobs was to get up on the conning tower as extra lookouts.

We came to action stations at dawn off the west coast of Greece. Gamp had been surveying the little ports and harbours we passed on the way to this patrol area and he seemed to be looking for something in particular. Officers working on the plotting table just in front of me noted down the smoke haze and shipping he reported, all speaking in a normal tone of voice, quiet, careful, competent and a world away from the parade ground bellowing we were used to. Then five or six ships were seen leaving harbour in company with three destroyers. This could be the convoy we are after, a really tasty target, so Gamp gets on the intercom to tell everybody what's happening, to stay on their toes and no bloody smoking. We turn south to track the convoy, steering to make the best of our poor speed.

After several quick glimpses through the periscope, doubts begin to creep in. These ships are not quite large enough, they simply do not fit the picture Gamp was expecting, yet they are heavily escorted. There is much discussion between the officers over the plotting table, with me earwigging like mad while trying to fade into the bulkhead. Reference books appear with silhouettes of ships, and these are compared with the intelligence information Gamp is working from. He finally decides this cannot be the right convoy, it might even be a decoy

47

set to draw away the likes of us. There are bigger fish to fry and he orders reverse course, turning down this opportunity in the hope of a better one further north.

Then smoke is sighted on the horizon. We are still submerged, so far too slow to get close enough to see the ships making it. Gamp backs his hunch and we follow the projected track of this other, north-bound convoy at our best speed for the rest of the day, willing it to get dark. Gamp uses the intercom again, tells them what's happening, and anyone caught smoking will be walking home. As soon as it's dark enough we surface and pound after the convoy. We are getting close to Corfu, where the heavily defended anchorage between the island and the mainland can only be approached through a narrow channel. Still on the surface but instantly ready to dive, we feel our way in.

Signals are flashed at us from both shores but we ignore them and motor steadily on following the channel until an E-boat, one of the large, powerful German motor torpedo boats, is sighted. Dive! Silence returns as we sit on the bottom and listen to propellers passing overhead, a strange, whooshing, rushing noise like a watery steam train. We sit tight for fifteen minutes then gingerly surface again only to sight a trawler patrolling the harbour mouth. Dive! Sit on the bottom listening, then rise gently to the surface again. This war of nerves is only just beginning – give me gunfire every time.

We finally enter the inner harbour, the anchorage itself, at periscope depth so only Gamp knows what's out there. We hang there for a while just submerged as he scans the horizon then decides to surface, where we wallow for a couple of hours running the diesels to charge the batteries. Lights on shore show people moving about but nobody takes any notice of us. Then we dive and sit on the bottom waiting for daylight.

Action stations at eight. Rise ever so slowly to periscope depth, and the good news is that Gamp was right to follow his instincts yesterday. The two very large supply ships he was looking for are moored alongside with a destroyer at anchor nearby – three fat targets. The technicalities of setting and firing torpedoes go over my head but they are fired at last, two towards the destroyer and four at the supply ships. Gamp wastes no time in running for the entrance, turning the boat while the stop-watches used to time the torpedoes tick away.

Sadly it seems we must have missed the destroyer, but as the officers are shaking their heads three enormous thumps come through the water, making the boat shudder. Gamp risks a quick look through the periscope and confirms that both supply ships are hit and sinking. I'm standing there grinning like everybody else as if I had done something to help, it was a very exciting moment, believe me, but I had no idea what was coming. Gamp raps orders, watertight doors are double clamped, everything loose is secured and everybody is looking for something to hold on to.

All we have to do now is get away. We are running as fast as we can for the channel which is nowhere near fast enough, no better than six or seven knots. Once again the sounds of many propellers come closer and cross over us, and the pounding begins. During that very long day we count no fewer than forty depth charges. These horrible things go off with a massive concussion that shakes everything, long after the boat that dropped them is out of earshot . All I can do is pull a face at Jock across the control room and hang on. There is nothing more frightening than being depth-charged when all there is to do is to hold on tight and look brave.

This very dangerous game of cat and mouse is played on our part by violent course changes, sudden stops and even reverse power. The enemy have the advantage, of course, they know we must make for the channel and the open sea, and aircraft are in the game now and they drop depth charges too. It's getting on for evening, at last, and Gamp risks periscope depth to get a fix on a landmark, to make sure we are where we think we are. One thing he does glimpse is a trawler chuffing across the main channel ahead of us, towing a boom that probably floats an anti-submarine net underneath. The officers, who look as shattered as I feel, calmly discuss this. The question seems to be whether we should surface and sink the trawler by gunfire, at which I perk up a bit. At least I will have something to do instead of just standing here dying for a leak. They finally decide to go the other way, to dive as deep as they can and try to run under the net.

The trawler's propeller noise recedes as we clear the entrance, make a violent course change and stay down until well after dark. A few hours later we have resumed our patrol, on the surface and charging batteries, where

Jock and I are on the conning tower breathing air so fresh you could bottle it, but we cannot talk. We were both stone deaf for hours.

As I have said, Gamp Miers won the Victoria Cross for this action, and every man of his crew was decorated. When the news of the decorations came through, he organized a dinner for the crew at the Fleet Club, and Jock and I were tickled pink to be invited. We didn't get any medals – no surprise there, neither of us had done anything except keep out of the way – but I would gladly exchange a dozen medals for a promise that I will never, ever be depth-charged again.

Chapter Six

Landings

Many of our trips to the Greek islands in the Aegean Sea involved the landing and sometimes the recovery of secret agents. The first time I had to do this came as a complete surprise. Bill Severn and I had been at sea on board HMS *Triumph* for a few days, all calm and normal, when the skipper collared me and said, 'We'll be landing your passenger tonight, Fee, so get your gear sorted, will you?' It was news to me that I had a passenger and I said so. Apparently this man dressed in civvies had dashed aboard from a car in Alexandria, dived into the cabin and had not come out since. The crew knew about him but had not said anything to us because they thought we did too. We talked it over with the skipper who was not much wiser than we were. All he knew was that this man had to go ashore at a certain place within a certain time and that we were going to take him there. Secrecy is all very well but it can land you in it sometimes. We only had our two-man Folboat aboard.

The torpedo room housed six spare torpedoes just behind the bow torpedo tubes where they could be quickly reloaded, and our gear, four kit bags holding the Folboat, weapons and explosives, was usually stowed in there. Even this modest amount of equipment had to be squeezed in. If the skipper had fired a few torpedoes and reloaded the tubes there was just enough space for us to assemble the Folboat before we surfaced, ready to shove it straight out through the hatch and into the water. Otherwise we had to put it together on the casing while the sub was surfaced.

On this occasion there was some elbow room, so Bill and I put the Folboat together and tried to work out how to fit three people into it. Bill found the answer. By removing the front seat he could get in and shove his legs right up into the bows, making enough room for the passenger to sit behind him with his legs either side. I could sit in the back seat as usual. We tried it for size with one of the torpedo room matelots and it seemed to work all right, but when I explained it to our passenger he was not impressed. His English was not very good (a lot better than my Greek, mind you, which was mostly the rude words the lads on the *Papanikolous* had taught us) but he was very doubtful. I made it clear it was this or swim and he had to lump it.

After dark we went through the usual landing routine. The skipper had a long, careful look through the periscope for signals from the shore, then surfaced the sub about half a mile out. We passed the Folboat out through the torpedo hatch and lowered it into the water, resting on the forward hydroplane. A couple of matelots held the painters fore and aft while we slid down the casing, caught the gear thrown down by some other matelots and stowed it in the boat.

Then our passenger appeared, wearing a belted raincoat and trilby hat and carrying a brief case, for all the world as if he was about to catch the eight-fifteen to London Bridge. Bill got in, the passenger was helped down and climbed in behind him and we paddled for the beach while the sub disappeared. The signal ashore was still flashing so there was no doubt about where to go. It was not particularly choppy and we took the usual care to paddle silently, but the boat was deep in the water and we were soon shipping quite a bit.

When we arrived at the beach the only thing our passenger could do was moan about his wet trousers. At least I think that was what he was moaning about, and they were certainly wet. A bunch of locals appeared, gathering round him sympathising and looking daggers at us. He went off with them, still moaning. Some people – and not even a tip for the driver! Bill and I stood there smiling and nodding at a couple of the locals who had stayed behind, and they stood there smiling and nodding back at us, none of us with the faintest idea what to do next. In the end we launched the Folboat and paddled out to sea to find the sub after the usual hour of blind man's buff, and carried on as if nothing had happened.

We spent most of our time either under water or in the dark, so when we did manage to get into the open air in daylight we looked pale and wan, despite the fact we had been in Africa for nearly a year. We became very sensitive about suntans, or rather the lack of them. Not having a suntan could lead to some serious misunderstandings.

If we went ashore and didn't fancy the Fleet Club it was almost inevitable that we would end up in a bar with a few Australians. Picture the scene: we are sipping our beer, the bits you could see of us under our baggy white shorts and huge pith helmets a delicate shade of pink; along the bar are some deeply tanned Aussies, fresh from the desert, wearing khaki drill scrubbed white and shorts like jock straps. Nobody enjoys a tear-up more than an Aussie with a few beers inside him, any excuse will do and we've just provided one. Seconds away.

They eye us up and begin to pass funny remarks between themselves. When that doesn't work they make loud comments about 'lilywhites' and ask each other where they could get a nice fresh pair of pink knees like those. That was our cue to start up a loud conversation about how hard life must be when you are the son of two strangers and will never know who your father was. It usually wasn't long after that before the fists began to fly, at which point the bar owners would always call the MPs. More than once it ended up with us and the Aussies fighting the law, until we learned that if we had the fight in the street the barmen would just shrug and let us get on with it. So when the fisting was about to start we would all troop outside, settle a few scores, and minutes later be back in the bar buying each other drinks and playing two-up, the best of pals.

Bill Severn and I were rostered for a job and got all our gear aboard *Triumph* while it was still daylight. About an hour before we were due to leave the duty officer sent for me and presented me with an order from Tommy Langton. I was to go to Tobruk now, straight away, instantly, no hanging about. Respect counted far more than rank in a small group like ours and Tommy and I got on like a house on fire even though he was an officer. I knew he probably had some half-baked scheme in mind, one that was likely to do me no good at all, but that was only the half of it. Tobruk was under siege and a highly dangerous place, while *Triumph* was about to leave. Bill and I talked it over with Major Courtney. An order was an order, but what about the submarine trip? It was finally decided that I would join Tommy in Tobruk and Bill would go with *Triumph* on his own. There was no one else to take my place at short notice and he would simply have to cope single-handed with anything that came up. It wasn't ideal, but that was what happened.

I grabbed some spare kit and made it aboard one of the ships in a small convoy that was going to sneak into Tobruk without the Jerries noticing. Some hopes. We were dive-bombed several times and there is little comfort in being dive-bombed when you are sitting on an ammunition ship. It's still a lot better than being depth-charged, at least you can shoot back. Some of the ships were hit but mine got into Tobruk harbour just after dark the next day. It was, as I had expected, quite a lively town. I set out to find Tommy with shells, spent

The boxing brothers c.1937:
Albert Feebery, 22,
professional middleweight,
and ...

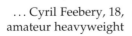

... Cyril Feebery, 18,
amateur heavyweight

Cpl B Walker's squad, Grenadier Guards, October 1937

Changing guard, Windsor Castle, 1938

Barossa Barracks, Aldershot, September 1939

ree volunteers for the Folboat Section: Feebery (left); John Riley (centre); and Andy Seddon (right)

A run ashore – Alexandria, 1941: John Riley, Feebery and Jock Booth

Wedding Day, 1943

'Feebery's Marauders', 1944: Feebery (third from left) and Bob Francis (extreme right)

A Jeep prepared for patrol, 1944

Feebery and the
liberated Buick, 1944

bullets and shrapnel from anti-aircraft rounds flying in all directions.

He had set up shop with the crew of a Motor Torpedo Boat and was working on a plan to attack the little Arab boats the Germans were using to resupply their forces. Dozens of them, about the size of a ship's lifeboat, had been commandeered and were coming into the beaches behind their lines every night with food and ammunition. Tommy had also been told to evaluate a new weapon and his current bright idea was to combine the two jobs.

'Sticky bombs' were the sort of brilliant new weapon that sounds fine in theory but that can create real problems in practice. They came two to a box that also held the handles and instructions for priming and so on, and were originally designed as anti-tank weapons. The fuse in the handle was primed and shoved into a hole in the bomb itself; removing a pin allowed the bomb's outer cover to fall away; and to finally make the thing live you pulled a tape out of the handle. They weighed about three pounds and looked like giant toffee apples or Christmas puddings with handles.

When thrown they squashed and stuck fast to whatever they hit, then went off ten seconds later. The really dangerous part was that once the cover fell away the bomb would stick to anything, and once they stuck they went off ten seconds later, whatever they were stuck to. In practice they could be as lethal to friend as to foe.

Tommy's plan sounded fine. We would stand right in the bows of the MTB, right on the sharp end in front of the torpedo tubes with a box of bombs ready on the deck. Having sighted one of the Arab boats the skipper would put his foot down and stampede up to it, and while he was doing that we would each assemble a bomb, lob them into the target as we shot past and be well away before they went off. We stooged around the harbour next day practising on planks and other junk floating around.

The first surprise was the sheer power of the MTB, which was driven by three huge aircraft engines and could accelerate to more than forty miles an hour in no time flat. The first time the skipper opened up those engines the bows lurched into the air, throwing us both off our feet to go tumbling back along the deck. The matelots enjoyed that. They even gave us a ripple of applause.

We went out that night to give it a try. It was breezy and the sea was choppy but sure enough there were lots of little Arab boats around creeping along close inshore. We were creeping along too, throttled right back as we looked for one to sink. Tommy went back to the bridge to point one out to the skipper, telling me to stand by. I had the handle of a bomb primed and ready to stick in, when Tommy ran back and our engines roared. The bows reared up just as they had in the harbour and we were ready for that, but then they crashed down again, then up, then down, rising and falling a clear eight feet every time as we hurdled from wave to wave across the choppy sea. It was impossible to stand in the bows without holding on, but you need both hands to fuse a sticky bomb. This first attack fizzled out in howls of laughter, leaving behind a boatload of no doubt very puzzled but very lucky Jerries.

Our next try was better organized. This time I stood while Tommy was sitting down holding a primed bomb. As we stormed towards another little boat I took the bomb handle with my free hand while Tommy drew the pin to shed the cover and ripped out the tape. The first throw missed so we turned round for another go and this one landed plumb in the boat. The MTB roared away with the two of us loudly counting down from ten, but nothing happened. It didn't go off.

This was all happening only a hundred yards from a beach that was enemy territory and we were attracting attention. Jerry was taking pot shots at us so the skipper headed out to sea having risked his boat enough for one night. We went back to Tobruk for a bite to eat, having decided that this was not a potentially valuable use of sticky bombs. When Tommy and I got back aboard *Medway* I asked after Bill Severn, wondering how he was getting on with all those nasty sailors pulling his leg and no-one to hold his coat. They told me that HMS *Triumph* had been sunk by enemy action while on patrol, with no survivors.

Chapter Seven

Crete

Allied submarines, MTBs and destroyers based at Malta were perfectly placed to attack Axis shipping. The island lay astride the enemy's easiest and most direct route between Italy and Africa, and the Jerries set out to capture it, putting the island under siege with round-the-clock air raids and attacks on our relief convoys when they tried to break through. Axis air forces based in Italy and Crete were enormous while none of our planes had the range to make a fight of it. Very few allied ships ever got through to Malta and without food, for the civvies as well as the soldiers, fuel and ammunition the island would have to surrender. The next Malta convoy simply had to get there.

The Folboat section were briefed to raid a number of German aerodromes on Crete. The intention was to destroy as many enemy aircraft on the ground as possible and so relieve some of the pressure on the Malta convoy. My party was led by Captain Kealey, and together with Lieutenant Allott and Jenks Jenkins we were to raid the airfield at Maleme. John Medley was attached to our party. He was a Sergeant in the armoured corps who had been captured during the fighting in Crete the previous year, escaped from the Italian prisoner of war camp and lived in the mountains with the partisans until he met a Folboat section raiding party who brought him back. He volunteered to show us the way to Maleme where he had been made to work as a PoW, and knew the area well.

The dear old *Papanikolous* had been allocated to take us to Crete. My heart sank when I thought just how old and rickety this boat had been when I last saw her, but we were welcomed on board like long lost brothers and she got us there and back, so it goes to show you cannot always tell by appearances. The plan was to land on the south coast of Crete and walk across to Maleme on the north coast, which sounds easy enough until you see the chain of rugged mountains that runs east-west the length of the island.

Months of riding around in submarines is not the best preparation for strenuous mountain walking and we all took it hard to begin with. Captain Kealey was in trouble early on, he simply wasn't up to it, to say nothing of coming on the job in a pair of brand new boots that he had not even broken in. His feet were a raw mess after a few hours so we left him in a village and pressed on with Lieutenant Allott in charge, a very down to earth officer who left you in no doubt where you stood.

John guided us straight to the aerodrome and we spent the last hour of daylight taking a long look at it. It was defended like a fortress, sandbagged gates, high and well kept wire fences, keen looking sentries patrolling with dogs. Mr Allott's concise appreciation of the situation was, 'This is a waste of bloody time!' but we had come all this way and had to have a go. We left John on the hillside with the gear and went in to do the job, walking straight into an anti-aircraft gun site we had not spotted from higher up, and were challenged by the sentry. We ignored him and tried to work our way round, but the cat was well among the pigeons by now. Sirens started wailing, lights came on all round the airfield perimeter, trucks began driving about inside. Needless to say, we legged it.

We found out much later that one of the other raiding parties, a mostly French mob which included Major the Earl Jellicoe, had attacked their target a day early, putting the defences on all the other target aerodromes in a high state of alert. Surprise was our strongest weapon and this time we had truly blown it. Jerry chased us back into the mountains and didn't spare the manpower. We were pushed and hustled and never given a moment's peace even at night. They combed the hills for us using spotter planes and vast numbers of troops, and it was touch and go several times.

Captain Kealey was still at the village and fit to move but he had also collected eight New Zealanders, more escaped PoWs, who wanted to come with us. Somehow this vast crowd of men made it to the rendezvous on the coast without alerting the Jerries. Leaving them in hiding, Jenks and I climbed down to the beach to check over the two Folboats and the little inflatable dinghy we had hidden there on landing, but they had gone. The cache of food we had been relying on for a couple of days had also disappeared.

We made signals out to sea that night and were mightily relieved to see a brief answering flash from the sub, but we could only sit among the rocks knowing that *Papanikolous* was out there stooging about waiting for us. They would be back tomorrow night so it was no great sweat. We collared some locals in the cold and hungry light of dawn and asked a few pointed questions. Captain Kealey could sling the bat and we soon discovered the boats and the grub in the nearby village, where their apologies rang a bit hollow. Back among the rocks with enough to feed ourselves and our flock of Kiwis, we stayed out of sight and spent the rest of the day eating and dozing and waiting for it to get dark.

The weather was breaking and the sea was cutting up rough but we got afloat. We put three men in each Folboat with a couple hanging on over the side, and I had one man with me in the dinghy, sitting on my legs while I paddled. We quickly lost touch with the Folboats because the dinghy was skidding about all over the place in the stiff breeze. I paddled around for about an hour without finding the sub, which was no surprise. I would have been amazed if we had found it first go, but the Kiwi was new to this game and got very agitated. I reckoned the dinghy had drifted a good couple of miles from where we had started, where the sub would be looking for us, but there was plenty of darkness left.

When I told him our best bet was to go back to the beach, get our bearings and start again he threw a fit. We went even so, landed, and carried the dinghy between us back along the beach until we came to a spot where a long sand spit ran out into the sea. It was just under water but by wading out as far as we could we had a head start with no drifting.

Once again I paddled out into the oggin, keeping as straight a course as I could by the stars and looking back at the loom of the mountains against the sky. When I thought we had come far enough off shore I stopped paddling every few minutes to listen for engines. My passenger was nearly in tears after a couple of hours of this and in his shoes I dare say I would have been the same. We had been chatting and he was a very nice chap who desperately did not want to be a prisoner again.

It was a great relief to both of us when the faint sound of a heavy engine came across the water. In fact it was such a relief to the Kiwi that he stood up, yes, he actually stood up on my legs in the dinghy, and began striking matches. I don't know how he had kept them dry but he was striking them and holding them up in his cupped hands and yelling for all he was worth. I thought about telling him that it might be a Jerry E-boat, which also had diesel engines, but decided not to.

It was the *Papanikolous* and they had already recovered the others. They helped us on board, taking the Kiwi below but I couldn't move. I had been sitting for hours with his dead weight on my legs and I simply couldn't feel them, so the Greek matelots had to drag me up the casing and lower me down the hatch by main force before the sub could dive. I had pins and needles for hours but that didn't matter, we were on our way home.

Our raid was a washout but other raids had succeeded in destroying enemy aircraft. I don't know whether it made any difference to the Malta convoy. Some ships got through. The Kiwis, Jenks, John and me had a run ashore in Alexandria, and we tried to talk John into joining us but he wouldn't have any of it. He said he would rather ride around in a tank any day which seemed very odd. Noisy things, tanks. Unreliable, too, as we were about to find out.

Chapter Eight

Under New Management

A month or two before the Crete raids a few of us were at HMS *Saunders* at Kabrit on the Great Bitter Lake when a convoy of trucks drew up on the open ground next door and a bunch of men jumped out. We took an interest, thought we recognized some of them and got chatting through the fence. We soon realized that we knew quite a lot of them either from 8 Commando or Layforce. They were now the Special Air Service and were here to set up a base camp, but they only had the trucks and their personal kit, and had been told to use their initiative. I happened to mention that the New Zealand battalion camped along the road a way were out on exercise for a few days and quite soon, as if by magic, the SAS had a fully equipped base camp up and running. Goes to show you shouldn't leave things lying around.

The reason for mentioning this is that our new-broom General Montgomery wanted all 'the funnies', as he called us specialist operators, brought under a unified command. Overnight, or so it seemed , we stopped being the Folboat Section and became the Special Boat Section. Then overnight again we came under the command of David Stirling as D Squadron Special Air Service. Confused? Tell me about it. It is very confusing to go on a submarine sortie belonging to one unit and come back to find that you now belong to a mob you have never heard of. As far as I was concerned at the time I was a member of SBS attached to SAS and that's what I have told people ever since.

The first job I went on as a member of Special Boat Section attached to Special Air Service was the big raid on Benghazi in September 1942. This grew from an incident when Stirling and two or three others drove into the town at night by bluffing their way past the Eyetie sentries while openly wearing British uniforms, then strolled around Benghazi docks eyeing the ships and wishing they had a boat and some limpet mines. It was so easy that Stirling went back twice more with Folboats and inflatables, but the boats let him down having been damaged during the long desert journey. The raid I took part in was his fourth attempt to attack Benghazi and involved more than 200 men, many of them like us, complete novices at desert raiding.

It was the biggest raid ever mounted by the SAS and it felt wrong from the start because of the numbers involved. The whole success of raiding forces like the SBS and SAS depended on small groups striking where they were least expected. Surprise was our most powerful weapon but I have read since that the plans for

67

the raid were the talk of Cairo before we left, which inevitably meant the Jerries knew as much about it as we did.

We were divided into three groups travelling independently. The first two groups were experienced SAS men whose task, among others, was to clear the way into Benghazi for us, the third group of inexperienced SAS men. Our task was to go straight through to the harbour, launch our Folboats and sink the ships. Our group was made up of about twenty trucks and half a dozen jeeps; sixteen of us ex-Folboat section men had four three-ton trucks to carry all the gear we would need for a long desert journey plus our Folboats, limpet mines and so on. A couple of SAS soldiers gave us a few tips on desert travel before we left but it wasn't nearly enough to prepare us for the real thing. We loaded up with no idea of where we were going until we were well out into the desert.

To reach Benghazi from Kabrit we had to drive about 800 miles south to a place called Kufra, cross a narrow section of the Great Sand Sea then drive north another 800 miles back to the coast. I guess when most people think about deserts they think of vast, hot, empty places covered with rolling sand dunes and the odd camel and palm tree here and there. In fact the desert we drove through was mostly stark and rocky, more often shingle or fine stones than loose sand; there are many different kinds of sand, too, ranging from the very firm to the very soft. Then there are sudden deep, steep sided valleys called wadis, ancient water courses that can take a lot of time and effort to cross. Rocks punctured oil sumps and tyres, trucks sank to their axles in soft sand and had to be dug out, and although they were three-ton trucks they were usually loaded with four tons of gear and half a dozen men. Driving across desert wasn't easy and we learned the hard way, but we learned enough to keep going.

Our group also had two advantages. The first was Sergeant Bernie Thorn and his team of mechanics. With more than eighty vehicles making the raid, the mechanics' job was to rescue and repair any that came to grief, and their trucks were loaded with tools and spare parts. We learned a lot from them, but our second advantage was the tanks.

These were two brand-new American-built light tanks officially called the Stuart although everybody called them 'Honeys'. Stirling had wangled them from somewhere with the idea they could smash through road blocks on the way to the harbour. A couple of Bernie's men had been trained to drive them and they rolled along with us most of the way. Just as well, because most of us would never have got there without them. Bernie's trained men soon got fed up with it and he asked if any of us would like to relieve them. There was no lack of volunteers to begin with but after a while everybody had something more interesting to do. The driving itself wasn't difficult, not in the wide open desert at any rate, but the noise of the engine inside that thick steel box was deafening – and the heat! Even with every hatch wide open it was cooking hot, and a couple of hours was all any man could stand.

On firm terrain the trucks would spread far apart on either side of the lead jeep, staying in sight of each other but well out of other people's wheel ruts, always looking for the hardest going. You could sometimes work up to a good fifty or sixty miles an hour for hours on end, then you would hit a soft patch and the truck would plough in. Every truck carried two eight-foot long sand channels, steel runners that had to be dug into the sand under the rear wheels to spread the weight and give the tyres some purchase. As the wheels rolled off, the channels would often go flying like two enormous arrows and somebody had to collect them and bring them back on board ready for the next time. On really soft sand the truck might only make few yards before it bogged down again and the whole process had to be repeated, sometimes for hours on end. It was very hard work, but we had the tanks.

Being tracked vehicles the tanks could make their way through sand where a wheeled vehicle would bog down, and it seemed like a good idea to use the tanks to tow the trucks out. Each tank was fitted with a built-in fifteen foot long tow chain with a large hook at the end, so the towing part was simple enough. The complication came when the truck was out and running on the surface, where it had to keep going or it would almost certainly bog down again. We had to work out a way to slip the tow chain so the truck could steer round the tank and drive ahead without stopping or losing traction.

The only way we could do this was to have a man crouching on the front bumper of the truck, holding on to the radiator cap with one hand. As the truck was dragged free and got moving it would catch up with the tank, slackening the tow chain enough for the man on the bumper to reach down with his free hand and slip the hook. It worked most of the time. The truck only had to hit a rock or slide sideways to throw off the man on the bumper. Then again, both drivers had to know what they were doing, because if the truck caught the tank up too fast, the hook-slipper became the meat in the sandwich if he didn't jump first. It was another job for which the supply of volunteers dwindled rapidly, but we would never have kept up with the timetable for the raid if it had not been for the tanks.

It was shame they didn't make it to Benghazi; they would have been useful, but it was not to be. On one stretch of good going the men driving them were larking about and they crashed. They had thousands of square miles of trackless desert to muck around in and they ran into each other. Bernie wrote off one tank then and there, while the other was so damaged that it only covered a few more miles before it had to abandoned.

We were in the hills outside Benghazi, pleasantly green and wooded hills, incidentally, not a bit like the desert we had just crossed, before Captain Allott explained the job in detail. It didn't take a genius to realize we were after ships, but which ships and where had been a mystery until now. We were told to load all our gear on two trucks ready to set off after dark, when the SAS would lead the way to the docks for our party

71

to launch Folboats and set limpet mines on whatever shipping we could find.

It took a very long time to find our way down the hillside to the road, where we drove in convoy, well spread out without lights, behind four SAS jeeps. The road was no more than ten feet wide with ditches either side. When the jeeps stopped for some sort of hold up in front so did we, and we sat there with the engines ticking over for some time when suddenly all hell broke loose. Machine gun fire, mortar rounds, all sorts of crap came flying towards us. In seconds the whole Folboat section were out of the truck and into the ditches. I wasn't the first but I certainly wasn't the last. A truck loaded with primed limpet mines is no place to be when bullets are flying around and we had nothing we could shoot back with. Nobody did this to us in our submarines.

This is where the tanks would have come in useful, but the SAS jeeps were returning fire and the Eyetie hate was dying down. Colonel Stirling, immaculate in Guard's officer's greatcoat and cap, strolled through it all to have a word with Mr Allott and explain what the hold up was. The Italians had barred the road, mined the fields on either side and prepared this reception, obviously expecting us. The SBS were no longer wanted and we were told in no uncertain terms to push off and return to base. That was easier said than done with no navigator and very little food or fuel. We retired in reverse gear for a few miles until we found a place where we could turn and get a move on. There wasn't much darkness left so we huddled into some sand dunes, camouflaged the trucks and spent the day keeping out of sight. We made it to the desert proper the following night, by which time we were nearly out of petrol. The trucks, still piled high with completely useless Folboats and anti-shipping mines, were hidden once more and we settled down to wait. Not much else we could do.

Next day we heard the sound of a jeep and came out from under the trucks where we had been lying in the shade. It was Captain Ford and Sergeant Cooper, chasing remnants – that was us. The whole operation had been called off and SAS units were making their way back to Kufra. They offered to go to a supply dump and bring back enough fuel and water for us to reach it, always supposing no one had emptied it in the meantime, so it was back under the trucks for another three days. They came back with petrol and one jerry can of water that tasted of petrol. They also had some fags which pleased Johnny Riley no end, he being a chain smoker who had run out two days ago. 'Anyone want a fag?' says Cooper, and Riley was out from under our truck like a whippet.

We set off that night in one truck, abandoning everything else, and ran for fifty miles or so, stopping before dawn to set up camp, camouflage and eat. Our acting cook set up the cooker, which was simply the two sand channels from the truck pushed edgeways into the sand about a foot apart, with a couple of pints of petrol poured onto the sand between them; drop a match in there and you've got a cooker. This man had done the job before so I don't know why it went wrong this time, but while we were all busy with other things he suddenly started screaming. He was only wearing shorts and sandals like the rest of us and was burned to a crisp across his chest, face and arms. All we could think of was that he had been standing downwind when he dropped the match.

We laid him in the shade and gave him first aid but he was in a very bad way. What to do next? If we took him with us he might last a few days in agony before he died. It might be easier on him if we simply left him where he was when we moved in the evening, but that was something Mr Allott flatly refused to consider. Then a man called Colclough volunteered to stay with him. He would try to get him back to the coast road to get help from the Jerries or the Eyeties. That's what happened in the end. Colclough stayed with the burned man and I have never seen or heard of either of them since.

It was some time before I got involved in another trip up the desert but at least we all had a decent suntan for once. The next job also called for Folboats and limpet mines so it was clearly another harbour, but which one? Alamein was being fought and the Jerries were making up their minds to fall back, so any attack on their supply lines would be a shrewd move. The route was much the same as before and there was all the same fun of digging the trucks out of sand, but without the tanks to make it easier. Only this time we headed much further west before approaching the coast, with a much greater chance of meeting enemy air or ground patrols. We were using a captured Italian truck, armoured at the front and fitted with a rail all round the sides that sloped up to run across the top of the armour plate where the windscreen should be. This rail carried two Breda guns, more like light cannon or pom-poms than heavy machine guns, that could slide along the rail so as to fire in any direction.

It is always a surprise to meet another vehicle in the desert. It's a big place. We had learned by now that the general rule was, if it's smaller than you, shoot at it, if it's bigger than you, run away. On this occasion we sighted an Italian truck very much like ours, decided it was smaller than us and turned towards it blazing away with the two Bredas. The Eyeties must have thought the same, and when we realized that our shells were bouncing off them like theirs were bouncing off us, we decided to go and get the cavalry. I slid my Breda along the rail to keep it on target as we turned, and as I locked it off to fire I felt a sharp pain in my left hand. Some of our other trucks were already coming to see what all the noise was about so we swerved off to one side hoping the Eyetie would follow us. He saw the other trucks and stopped, turned as they roared towards him and disappeared into the haze.

Now there was time to look I saw that the tip of my little finger was dangling. Whether it was enemy action or my own silly fault I will never know. I do know that I received no sympathy at all and some rough and ready first aid that included a piece of card torn from a fag packet as a splint. Two or three days later when we were assembling close to the objective, Tripoli, the doctor had a look at it and did it up properly. He insisted on a sling.

The SAS had been operating along the coast road for some weeks, raiding German supply convoys and gathering intelligence, and there were several men with light wounds like mine. There was also one man who kept wandering off talking to himself, another who kept a pet rat in his jacket and talked to it, and yet another who wouldn't say anything to anybody, man or rat. They had just had enough and were ready to go home. David Stirling told me in his usual direct way that I was no use to the raid and to take thirteen of these men back to our lines. I was allocated a rickety old truck and fourteen days' petrol and rations. Look after them, the Colonel said, take them back to hospital in Alexandria or to base at Kabrit. He couldn't tell me where the fighting was but told me to stick to the desert parallel with the coast until I judged it safe to make for the coast road. He also gave me a chit to GHQ where I was to report first.

The truck kept breaking down but one of the wounded men was an ace mechanic and kept us rolling. The first vehicle we had seen in nearly three weeks was a British armoured car that stopped thoughtfully on the edge of the haze and let us come closer. They could not have been in much doubt for long because my lot were standing up in the truck waving their shirts, cheering and whistling. We were passed through and joined the heavy traffic on the coast road near Sidi Barrani, most of which was heading west. We managed to scrounge some rations and water, and by showing the Colonel's chit at every opportunity I eventually found an officer prepared to guide us to GHQ. You cannot be surprised at their reluctance. We had not washed, shaved or taken our clothes off for far too long, but when we found the place I met an officer who knew all about Colonel Stirling and the SAS. Lieutenant General Bernard Montgomery read the chit, looked us over and spent the next five minutes telling us what a grand job we were all doing. That speeded up the paperwork no end.

I was given another dated chit which entitled me to draw three days' rations from the next supply dump, where it would be dated again for another three days, and so on until we got back along the five hundred or so miles of coast road to Alexandria. After all the effort the army had made to get supplies and fuel to where they needed them most they did not want too much going back the wrong way. Even so, my invalids were recovering with healthy appetites. We had been short of food for a week or more and managed to eat those three days' rations in the next twenty-five miles. It was getting dark and we were getting peckish when we came across another supply dump and drove in to try our luck.

The officer there was very understanding and let me talk him into giving us some more. We drove round the dump with him and a couple of his men to pick up a box of this, two bags of that and half a dozen tins of the other, while he sat in the cab ticking them off like a shopping list. We drove away into the dusk with another three days official rations on board, and when it got dark pulled off the road to brew up and kip.

It was then that I discovered what a disreputable lot

of soldiers I was in charge of. While the supply officer and his men had been carefully giving us our exact ration during our tour of their dump, every time we stopped my invalids had been slipping off the back to help themselves. Our rickety truck was groaning with everything they could lay hands on and we spent a happy evening finding out what they had 'won'. Suffice it to say there was no shortage of rations for the rest of the trip, and we ended up swapping stuff for beer and fags. What was left over came in very handy when we decided to spend a couple of days 'convalescing' in Cairo before reporting to Kabrit.

Chapter Nine

Seaborne Raiders

David Stirling was captured by the Germans late in 1942 and command of what was now 2nd SAS Regiment devolved to Paddy Mayne. With the end of the war in Africa not far away plans had to be made for the next phase. There would be plenty of scope for seaborne raiding forces through the length of the Mediterranean and D Squadron SAS became the Special Boat Squadron around January 1943. Our new CO was Major the Earl Jellicoe and his priority was the expansion of the unit. A training base was set up at Athlit in what was then known as Palestine, a lovely spot, a sheltered bay with an old Crusader castle crumbling on the headland and mountains nearby. Among the officers was Tommy Langton, now a Captain, and I was promoted Sergeant Major. A hundred men had volunteered for the SBS. We were given a few weeks to assess them and select fifty. Major Jellicoe then flew to England, leaving Tommy in charge.

The training followed a familiar pattern: swimming,

of course; PT and unarmed combat; fast marching with loads over rough country; navigation; weapons, ours and the enemy's; fuses, bombs and explosives; Folboats and inflatable dinghies; first aid; escape and evasion. Much of this was practised at night and Tommy and I had to be able to do it too, but how do you decide which fifty men to pick from one hundred? The only sensible answer is that it depends what you are looking for. They had to be physically fit, of course, and that had to include confidence in the water – when something went wrong in the SBS you usually ended up in the oggin. Determination, certainly, and the ability to think clearly and make sensible decisions despite pressure and fatigue. But there was something else, something to do with character and personality and wit and intelligence which is very difficult to define. All I can say is you knew it when you saw it. I dare say there are all sorts of scientific tests and check lists nowadays, but Tommy and I had to pick 'em and we made it up as we went along. I think we got it right more often than not.

The first few days began with a run out of camp along one arm of the bay to the point, a swim a quarter mile or so to the other point and a run back to camp. All the volunteers were supposed to be able to swim and this soon sorted out the men who could only doggy paddle, who were swiftly 'Returned To Unit' for their own sakes. The rest of the day took its course. The best thing about it was that we didn't have to break our necks whittling anybody to size. They were all volunteers, officers included, they were all given a fair go and if they didn't suit for any reason – RTU. Nobody lost anything, except perhaps a few seconds pride.

We weren't always so harsh. I can remember one man who was ideal in every way except that he was a weak swimmer. I spent time coaching him and trying to improve his confidence until he finally met the minimum requirement. He repaid the effort superbly, serving with distinction in the Aegean with the SBS and later in France with 1st SAS, where he was captured and executed by the Germans late in 1944.

After a couple of weeks of this we were getting down to the hard core, the sixty or so men who had done everything we asked them to and still came back, grousing, swearing and totally knackered but ready for more. They had earned a weekend off and things were quiet, so Tommy asked me if I fancied a bit of skiing. Now, I had known him a long time and we were always pulling each other's leg. Thinking this was yet another wind-up I played along, arranged for a jeep and the petrol, and waited for the sting. We had driven miles north, clear through Palestine to Syria and up into the mountains before I began to believe that he was on the level.

For once Tommy wasn't having me on. 9th Army had taken over a ski school in a hotel, dead posh, exclusively for officers, and he had wangled some rooms. The higher we climbed the colder it got. The road was packed snow, and we were wearing shorts and arrived shivering, so the officer in charge sorted out a couple of greatcoats for us. The dining room waiters and some of the other diners looked down their noses at me because I was only a Warrant Officer, but that was their problem and the grub was lovely. We spent a couple of days on the slopes, mostly falling over but eventually managing to slide downhill a bit first. As it got dark on the second day we returned to the hotel to find a message from Major Jellicoe ordering us back immediately, and we arrived at Athlit in the small hours next morning.

The panic was caused by the General commanding 9th Army, who had expressed an interest in us and wanted to inspect the base. I think it had something to do with the Major's trip to England and the wires he had been pulling while he was there. We had to prepare ourselves for an official visit and lay on demonstrations and so on, even if it did stand on our shovel as far as winning the war was concerned. When the great day dawned everyone was on top line. We had a PT squad standing by, another group on the beach ready to assemble Folboats, unarmed combat and small arms displays and so on. The General, whose name I think was Wilson, arrived surrounded by various brass hats and swarms of MPs and was duly received with bags of bull.

My place in all this was two paces behind Major Jellicoe as he welcomed the General. First thing was to introduce our officers and Tommy Langton was head of the line. The General was chatting to Tommy when he glanced along the line and there, a few men on, was Captain Randolph Churchill, who had turned up at Athlit the night before and fallen in with the officers when ordered to do so. The General dropped Tommy liked a hot brick and walked straight past our genuine officers to have a ten-minute chat with his pal, the Prime Minister's son. The look on Jellicoe's face was priceless. Randolph had gone that afternoon and luckily we did not see him again until Philipville, months later.

The men went through their paces, the General and his party were given lunch and left soon after having seen what they came to see. We waited respectfully while the General stood by the open door of his car having a long, quiet talk with Major Jellicoe before he drove away. We soon found out what that was all about. We had been thinking for some time that what the men needed to get them really on their toes was a good, realistic exercise, and the General had suggested that we might like to test the defences of 9th Army. We set about organising this as quickly as we could and, working with 9th Army staff, we devised Exercise Bronx that took place between 15 and 25 May 1943. Our men were divided into four groups, to be dropped off from trucks along the coast to simulate a seaborne landing. They would then work their way inland to attack targets by placing dummy bombs on them. There were pages of detailed instructions, identification passes printed in three languages, neutral umpires flown in from 1st Army, the works.

There had to be rules, as with any exercise, but we wanted to keep as much surprise as possible so we bent a few. What 9th Army Staff did not know were the targets, nor did they know that even before the planning began some of our old hands, dressed up as locals, were wandering around their territory looking for dumps and airfields we could attack.

Our men had to carry all their food and water as well as weapons, and they were each given ten carefully weighed bags of sand to simulate bombs. According to the exercise rules they were also required to wear red headbands to identify them as 'enemy' troops. These headbands were actually given out and the men were all wearing them when the trucks left Athlit, but I don't suppose they lasted long after that. Mine didn't.

This was all well under way when Major Jellicoe asked me which target I fancied. That was a bit of a stopper, because I had planned to swan round Syria in a jeep for ten days to keep an eye on the men, offering encouragement, bending the rules to our advantage, that sort of thing. Rank has its privileges, after all. When the Major went on to explain that he really wanted to stuff one up that toffee-nosed General, and did I feel equal to having a go at 9th Army Headquarters, well, you can't say no, can you? The only men left behind in camp were a few sick and injured, good lads doing 'light duties' as cooks and orderlies while they mended, so I had a wander round and soon found three willing volunteers. We kitted up and, a few hours after the main parties left camp, a truck dropped us about fifty miles short of the town where 9th Army headquarters was located.

This had to be as realistic as possible if these three men were to gain anything from it. The 'defenders' knew that raids were to be attempted during this ten day period and they were certain to be expecting us, so it was night marching by compass and the stars, laying up out of sight by day and a full day's observation of the target from the hills. The town was surrounded by a wall, so we would have to enter by one of the gates, which were all controlled by sentries. It was quickly obvious that men in uniform were passing through without a second glance while natives were being stopped and searched. Easy. We approached the town in the evening as things began to wake up after the heat of the day with me in the lead, two more twenty yards behind and number four twenty yards behind them. All we had to do was to stay spread out but in sight of each other and take it easy, mingle with the crowd and not call attention to ourselves.

As I came closer to the gate I spotted a very tall officer, a Captain, hanging about on the roadside, with the white band round his cap that marked him as an exercise umpire. Just what I needed at this ticklish moment but I cracked him a Guards salute.

'Sergeant Major Feebery?' says he, returning the salute and telling me his name which I've forgotten. 'I've been expecting you. I shall be the umpire for your raid, will you tell me what you intend to do?'

I wasn't sure myself, but one thing I certainly did not intend was have him walking around with us sticking out like a sore thumb. I asked him to move off the road out of sight of the sentries and he saw my point straight away. I also wanted to refill our dummy bombs. Realism or not, we had not carried ten bags of sand for

85

fifty miles when we didn't have to. I doubt if any of the men had, they weren't daft. The umpire agreed to trail us without crowding too close and was as good as gold. I asked him where the HQ was but he just laughed and told me it was somewhere near the centre of town, so we spread out again and went through the gate. The sentries didn't even look at us.

Crowds of people were milling about and it was falling dark among the buildings. I just followed my nose until we came to what just had to be Army Headquarters – a sandbagged gateway in a high brick wall, MPs on guard, cars and people going in and out with much saluting and showing of passes. It had to be, but I kept walking. A hundred yards or so further on, the high brick wall turned at right angles and disappeared along the side of a house. There was a whole row of houses and between them you could see the brick wall running along the bottom of their back yards. I signalled my team to get together in an entry between two houses while the umpire lounged innocently on the other side of the street.

One man stayed on watch in the entry while the rest of us slipped to the back of the house. Sure enough, there were lean-to sheds built against the high brick wall, and it was easy to shin up on the roof of one of them and look over into the compound. It was dark enough. The dummy bombs were tucked inside our jackets, while the rest of the gear was left on the shed roof. One rucksack lay on the wall so that we could find the right spot to get out again. Then one by one we dropped into

9th Army Headquarters, where by this time the lights were on in the barracks, the NAAFI was open, it was all just like home and we were just a few more squaddies strolling about. I looked back after fifty yards to see our umpire drop over the wall, then found a quiet doorway where we could watch and wait and get our bearings and the layout of the place in the last of the daylight.

Standing alone in one corner was a sort of tower with aerials sprouting out of the top and a flight of stairs leading to a door half way up. Communications – that had to be the place to go for. We talked it through in whispers. There were no guards or special precautions that we could see, so I detailed one man to wait at the foot of the stairs to stop anybody coming up in case we wanted to come down in a hurry. Then the rest of us walked up and through the door.

It was an office, and the Lieutenant sat behind the desk said, 'What's this? You can't come in here!'

'Can't I?' I said, dumping one of my 'bombs' plumb in the middle of his blotter. 'That's an explosive device. Don't touch it, it's primed to go off in three minutes. Now stand up and get over there!' Warrant Officers don't often get the chance to talk to pompous Lieutenants like that, not in public at any rate, and I was making quite a lot of noise. The other two had come in and shut the door so it didn't matter, but they nearly died of fright when the door opened again and the umpire stepped in. He was shaking his head and the look on his face spoke volumes. Then a Sergeant Major appeared down some stairs to see what all the noise was about and I told him his fortune as well: stand still, shut up, if this was real you would be dead. The umpire could only nod.

Our bombs were all over this room by now. Upstairs was the actual wireless room where several men were busily sending Morse code. We just dumped a 'bomb' in front of each of them, yelled, 'Don't touch it!' and left them to get on with it. The officer and SM were made to face the wall and the three of us and the umpire nipped out and down the stairs sharpish. Once in the compound we walked slowly away, spreading out as before. The worst thing you can do is run; it attracts attention.

We were well on the way back to our exit when the balloon went up. Sirens wailed, floodlights came on, MPs dashed about, everybody started shouting and doubling away somewhere, mainly towards the gates. The umpire stared in disbelief at the shambles four of us had caused while we hopped over the wall, collected our gear and were away between the houses. The umpire called out to me from the top of the wall, the clot, so I waited for him in the entry.

'I suppose you'll make for that gate, Mr Feebery?' he said, pointing to another of the many gates in the town wall at the end of the street. My plan was to go out through the gate we had come in by, back past the entrance to Army Headquarters. As far as I knew we had to make it to the coast and that was our direct route. He just nodded and we spread out and strolled away with the umpire tailing us as before. The HQ was a seething mass of soldiers by now, alarms and sirens were still going off, the whole place was in turmoil as we sauntered past, taking an interest but not stopping. Out through the gate unchallenged, even with all this going on, and we ducked into the bushes four hundred yards down the road to have a quiet celebration.

The umpire joined us and asked me what I planned to do, so I told him: walk to the coast. 'No, really, it's all right, Sergeant Major,' he said. 'As far as you are concerned the exercise is over now. I've laid on a truck to take you home, if you'll wait here a few minutes I'll organize it.' Sure enough, a little while later a truck pulled up and drove us all the way back to Athlit.

I got quite a bit of stick from Major Jellicoe for this, largely because he got it from the General. I was told it wasn't fair, I should have left notes explaining that those bags of sand were *not* explosive devices primed to go off in three minutes. 9th Army communications were screwed up for days before the bomb disposal experts declared the place safe. There were also some extremely red faces among the MPs responsible for security when they read the umpire's report, and certainly no love lost on the SBS. It wasn't bad for a trio of invalids either, and I cannot even remember their names. Afterwards I realized that if any of the men in that signal tower had been armed we could have been in dead lumber. It's also funny to think that if we had done it to the Germans or the Italians we would all four of us be heroes.

Chapter Ten

Sardinia

Having got the Italians and Germans out of Africa the next step would be to invade Europe somewhere and there were plenty of places to choose from. Diversionary raids were carried out the length of the Mediterranean to keep the opposition guessing while our brass hats made their minds up. A party of SBS were ordered to join 2nd SAS Regiment at Philipville in Algeria. About forty men were selected and we drove from Athlit to Alexandria, joined a seaborne convoy to Tripoli and completed the journey from there by road. Some of this party were old hands but a lot of them were new men who had never been on operations. Exercise Bronx did them the world of good but now they were going to get a taste of the real thing.

Major Jellicoe arrived and told me Tommy Langton would not be coming. He was in hospital getting over his last job, during which he walked nearly 400 miles across the desert back to our lines. Tommy and I next met in Scotland a year or more later, by which time we were both in the SAS again.

I was told to keep the officers and men occupied, so we set up a daily routine that began with a run along the beach, a decent swim, ten minutes PT, then run back for breakfast. The rest of the day passed with weapons training, important for us all because we had been issued with American M1 carbines, light automatic rifles, and we all had to get used to them. Some of the men had never trained with Mills grenades and a lot of them had never seen German grenades and other enemy weapons.

The old hands were quickly fed up with this. Apart from the new rifle they had done it all before, but we were confined to camp except for training. In an attempt to keep their minds on the job I had men who had been on operations give lectures about what they had learned. When Randolph Churchill turned up again he gave a talk on politics and the House of Commons.

A word about Randolph. As far as I know, no one has ever told the whole truth about this man, who may have been a good speaker but was a useless officer. During the short time he spent at Philipville, for instance, he came on our 'morning stretch' once, when he was trailed by his batman driving a jeep, into which he retired when the going got too tough for him. He was supposed to be in charge of picking us up from Sardinia after this raid, but I found out much later that by the time I got to the rendezvous he was in Yugoslavia. Best place for him.

Soon after we got to Philipville a letter from home caught me up, telling me that my brother was in Africa with 1st Army. Bert and I had only met once after the great falling out six years before, since when he had married and become a father, and volunteered as a despatch rider for the Royal Signals. At least the British Army could get something right – they were using an expert motorcyclist as a DR. He was now based at the Signals HQ in Constantine, about fifty miles inland. I asked the 2nd SAS signals officer to find out if there was any chance of getting in touch with him. He shrugged and pulled a face, but I never met a signals officer who didn't when asked a question like that. Next day a runner came to my tent, I was wanted urgently on the phone, and as I walked in the duty officer held out the receiver and said, 'Would you like to speak to your brother?'

Neither of us really knew what to say to each other, as usual. Bert wasn't the most talkative person at the best of times, unlike me, but it was great to hear his voice and bits of news from home. But that wasn't the end of it. A few days later, Major Jellicoe asked me to take an important document to signals headquarters in Constantine. Then he winked and said, 'You'd better organize yourself a driver, I want you back here in twenty-four hours!' Pat Scully, who really was an old soldier by our standards, with over twenty years service and pushing forty from the wrong side when I knew him, said he wouldn't mind a run. We scrounged a jeep and an hour or so later I was delivering this so-called important document to the Signals CO.

'Ah, yes,' he said, having read whatever it was, 'I believe your brother is with us. If you go to the canteen he'll meet you there.' Bert had been mystified to be given a twenty-four hour pass out of the blue that morning and he had been wondering how to spend the time. We had a meal and decided to go into town for a drink. Later – much, much later – Pat and I left Bert lying on the wall outside his quarters because we couldn't get the door open. Pat was in just as bad a state as me but he was here as the driver so I snugged down into the passenger seat and went to sleep.

I came to feeling lousy and freezing cold. It was pitch dark, the jeep was nose down in a sand dune and Pat was slumped over the wheel fast asleep. He took his time waking up but I managed to get him on his feet and we flagged down a passing truck. We were really parched, but after a few mouthfuls of water we were sloshed again – it's good stuff that anis, two hangovers for the price of one. The truck driver and his mate had to do most of the work but they dragged our jeep back on the road. We were miles off course and Pat drove, slowly, into Algiers where we ate something and cleaned up. It was late afternoon before we weaved into Philipville. We were not popular.

We knew things were warming up when we were transferred on board another submarine depot ship, HMS *Maidstone*, in Algiers harbour. Once aboard we were secure and could be briefed on the details of the raid, or rather, as many of the details as we needed to know. The targets for Operation Swann were four enemy airfields on Sardinia. Four groups of SBS men were to land from a submarine on the west coast of the island and attack the airfields from inland.

I never did a job with SBS or SAS that went entirely according to plan. However carefully you had thought things through beforehand, sooner or later something would happen that meant you had to start making it up as you went along. Five officers and twenty-four other ranks left Algiers on 27 June 1943 on board HMS *Tiber*, and although we didn't know it yet the plan for this raid had already gone off the rails.

There is no spare room on a submarine, as I have already said, and twenty-nine extra bodies and all their gear were a major intrusion, not least in taking up air space. Very soon after diving a lot of our men began to feel ill. We put it down to inexperience and seasickness at the time, but what we thought were 'first night nerves' were in fact the early symptoms of malaria. The camp at Philipville was notorious for vicious mosquitoes but it seems no one had connected this with the danger of malaria.

But then, we had only just started. After three days running, surfacing at night to recharge the batteries, the skipper reckoned he was at the right place. Two groups of men were to land here, one commanded by Captain Thompson and my party under Lieutenant Duggin. With much pushing and shoving and everyone trying to get out of the way we humped our bags and boxes onto the casing. There were many expressions of astonishment at the sight of me leading from the front, for once, and many fond farewells. I remember thinking that a lot of the men looked peaky, but it had been even more over-crowded than usual.

Sailors are generally a friendly bunch of people and in my opinion submariners are among the best, but they don't like hanging about on the surface. We inflated our dinghies on the casing, lowered them onto the forward hydroplanes and loaded the gear. You always got soaked doing this, especially when the matelots were chucking stuff down as fast as they can go, saying, 'There you are, mate, you'll be all right now!' as they disappear down the hatch. A few minutes later we were paddling across an empty sea with nothing but a few bubbles in sight. Amazing how quickly a sub could disappear, but I didn't have time to ponder it just then.

This sudden burst of activity in the fresh air left Sergeant McKerrica and Privates Thomas 401 and Thomas 501 in a bad way. I bullied them along, but when we reached the beach they could hardly stand. Even so, they tried to help with the unloading while Lieutenant Duggin and I went for a scout round and Private Noriega buried the deflated dinghies. Fifty yards inland was a cliff about a hundred feet high. We couldn't find a path up it, so I climbed it taking a rope with me. It was steep but made of very soft, crumbly stuff so it was easy to kick footholds and get a purchase. I tied the rope off round some scrubby bushes at the top and climbed down again. In the next couple of hours we shifted our gear from the beach to an overgrown spot about 200 yards inland from the cliff top. McKerrica and the two Privates had to be tied on and hauled up because they were all feverish by now, shivering one minute and sweating buckets the next. Five men from the two parties were ill and we finally realized it must be malaria. We made them as comfortable as we could and sorted ourselves out after a bit of a rest.

Meanwhile, I need to relate what happened on the submarine after we left it, because this is important to the rest of the story. While he was on his way to the next landing place the skipper saw that most of the soldiers left on board were very ill. He decided to abandon the operation and take them back to Algiers as fast as he could. Most of the men who should have landed on Sardinia that night were in hospital a few days after we left them. Our two groups were the only men to land from the submarine. Without any way of contacting us we were assumed to be as ill as everybody else and were simply written off. I found out much later that the operation was quickly reorganized and the airfields were raided by fresh teams that parachuted in, but of course we knew none of this at the time.

Captain Thompson set off with his group. Lieutenant Duggin waited to see whether McKerrica or either of the Thomases would recover enough to come with us, but after a couple of hours they were no better. It was decided to leave them where they were; they understood the job had to be done, and if they felt better inside forty-eight hours they were to follow us. If not they were to stay put for at least five days to give us a chance to do the job and get clear. That left the Lieutenant and I,

Private Noriega and an American Ranger named Louis Tronche who had come along as an 'observer'. We couldn't carry all the gear, so food and first aid stuff was ditched in favour of water, ammunition and explosives. In sharing out the extra I gave half a dozen Lewis bombs and their time pencils to Tronche, but he refused to take them, saying he didn't understand them.

'You don't have to understand them,' I said, 'you just have to carry them!' but he said no, he would rather not. I was fuming, but neither the Lieutenant nor I had any authority over him. He was a fluent Italian speaker, which might come in handy, but his commitment to the job was obviously in serious doubt. He seemed to be far more interested in contacting his relatives on the island than in destroying aircraft.

We started climbing and it was heavy going. The mountains of Sardinia are steep and covered in nasty bushes that do their best to cut you to ribbons. Our maps were not very detailed and we had to avoid every farm, village and major road to maintain surprise. Tronche was lost on the first day. I had had another go at him for bunching up too close and he took to the rear, childishly lagging hundreds of yards behind. We waited for him to catch up a couple of times, Mr Duggin had a word, but he just disappeared that afternoon and was seen no more until we got to the prisoner of war camp. We made a quick search at the time, decided he was no great loss, and the three of us pressed on regardless.

We came in sight of the airfield after three days and found a place to hide where we could observe it. By now the Lieutenant was in a bad way. He had malaria – I was becoming an expert in diagnosing it – and had been dragging himself up and down the mountains by sheer strength of will. Even so we had made good time and still had a full day in hand before the night of the raid, according to the original timetable that we were still following. Noriega and I put the Lieutenant to bed and started the long process of studying the target.

It was a busy aerodrome with aircraft of all sorts taking off and landing. Large fuel and ammunition dumps were dotted around the perimeter and we identified vehicle parks, workshops and barracks. There were few patrol movements as far as we could tell and only a flimsy wire fence between us and all those lovely aircraft. We ate the last of our food and bedded down in the bushes.

Next morning there seemed to be a lot more activity. Aircraft were taking off and flying low and slow around the aerodrome, while several groups of men seemed to be inspecting the fence and the dumps. The Lieutenant was still far from fit but crawled out of his sleeping bag to watch with us, as trucks began delivering huge coils of barbed wire around the perimeter, which squads of men then opened out inside the original fence to make a barrier we couldn't hope to cut through quickly with our simple hand tools. To make our day complete, as darkness fell every aeroplane on the field started up, taxied to the runway and took off until there wasn't one left.

Unknown to us, the substitute SBS/SAS teams had parachuted in and attacked the other target airfields the night before, giving rise to all the activity we had seen. Even the Eyeties weren't going to stand still and let us do up the one remaining operational airfield on the island. For me, it was Maleme all over again.

There was no point in hanging about and there might still be a chance of attacking the dumps. We packed up, the Lieutenant very shaky, and reached the road around midnight, following it around the perimeter fence past the admin buildings. There was nobody about and we could see stacks and piles of equipment under tarpaulins fifty yards inside, just begging to be blown up. Without decent wire cutters that meant finding a way in but we were having to stop every few hundred yards to let Mr Duggin rest.

That last walk did for him. It took all his energy just to stand upright, let alone walk, and we had not eaten for a day. After another rest I said to him, 'Time to move on, sir.' When there was no reply I leaned over to find him shaking and sweating.

'Sorry about this Sergeant Major,' he said, 'but I can't get up. You'll have to carry on by yourselves.'

I looked at Noriega. 'We can't just leave him here,' he said, so between us we got him to his feet, took an arm each and set off along the road once more. After a bit he said he was feeling better.

We were at the northern end of the airfield by now and sat in the undergrowth beside the road to talk the problem over. Our main targets had taken off and flown away. We had established that there was no easy way to reach the dumps, and only a couple of hours of darkness remained. We decided to attack the secondary target, a railway line, then make for the east coast and the rendezvous with the submarine.

We had been carrying six men's issue of explosive for several days and I was glad to be getting rid of it, even if it was only under a lousy railway line. We planted it all along half a mile of track, then set off in the last of the darkness to put some distance between ourselves and the milk train. It was the morning of 11 July and we had forty or so miles to travel.

Within a hundred yards Lieutenant Duggin collapsed, shivering violently. 'You'd better carry on,' he said, 'I'll catch you up later.' Then he started rambling and was obviously far gone. We couldn't leave him but we couldn't afford to hang about either. Noriega and I carried him back to the road, ducking when we heard a lorry coming. It drove past and stopped further up, and leaving the two of them in the ditch I crawled along to find out why it had stopped.

It was guard post, a hut beside the road that we had passed during our walk the night before. The driver was leaning out chatting to a couple of sentries. I waited till he drove off and the sentries went indoors. Crouching in the ditch, Noriega and I went through the Lieutenant's pockets, taking his maps and revolver. His water bottle was half full, so we bound the strap round his wrist where he couldn't miss it if he woke up and needed a drink, then shoved him into his sleeping bag. We carried him along the ditch as quietly as we could to within a few yards of the guard post. One of the sentries came out and dumped his shaving water in the ditch but didn't see us. As he turned his back we lifted the Lieutenant onto the grass verge, left him as comfortable as we could and legged it for the coast.

I met Mr Duggin after the war. He had been well treated by the Italians, then spent the rest of the war as a PoW in Germany, in and out of hospital all the time with malaria.

Five days later Noriega and I climbed the last ridge between us and the sea. We hadn't eaten for six days now and were living in hope that the submarine would be where it was supposed to be to pick us up. We both collapsed, sound asleep until six in the morning, then set off on the very last leg of the journey to the rendezvous. We were walking in a daze. Noriega was showing signs of malaria and I was wondering when my turn would come.

Chapter Eleven

Prisoner of War

We walked straight into a squad of Carabinieri. Never even saw them. Their officer was very excited. I found out later from Noriega, who spoke some Spanish, that they had been waiting for us at the RV for days. The officer had his men surround us while he searched us, removing my belt from which was slung a pair of .45 Smith and Wesson revolvers that I had won from an American in a card game back in Philipville. The Eyetie was tickled pink with them. 'Canone!' he shouted, waving the huge weapons around like John Wayne while his lads chuckled. They certainly outclassed his regulation peashooter.

Once they had had their fun they treated us pretty well. They gave us some food and a cigarette before chaining us together. Noriega was swaying as the malaria gripped him but we had to walk back some of the way we had come to a road, where a lorry took us all to the police station in Cagliari. This was 17 July. Noriega had a very bad bout of malaria that night but the Eyeties wouldn't give him any treatment or fetch a doctor. They had put us in separate cells and I had to sit there listening to him shouting and thrashing about without being able to do anything to help. On only one meal a day I was feeling pretty bad myself after our recent diet. I raised a stink next morning and they let me in to see him. They still wouldn't bring a doctor but they did let me wash him and feed him with a spoon. I was convinced he would die if they didn't do something to help but there was no way I could force them.

When they thought I was softened up enough I was interrogated by an Italian officer who told me that all our soldiers had been captured. He was so pleased with himself that he read me a list of their names and numbers, which was a mistake. I knew that most of the men on his list had been left behind in camp at Philipville when we went to the *Maidstone*, and they certainly weren't on board *Tiber*. It showed that something had gone seriously wrong with the original plan and that some major change had been made of which I knew nothing, so I clammed up even tighter.

I was very correct and gave my name, rank and number in parade ground tones to every question he asked, until he lost his temper and threatened to have me shot. I remember thinking that wasn't such a bad idea if the choice was to live under the control of these bastards. I did ask for a doctor for Noriega and he told me he would see about it, then I was marched out to an empty room and told to sit down. There wasn't much point in escaping in Sardinia (where would I go?) but as

I sat there I couldn't help thinking how easy it would be to drop out of the window and nip across the yard to that gate . . .

I was interrupted by a soldier who came in to guard me – at least that's what he told me, in perfect English. There followed some patter about the happy times he had spent in England and how he was dead against the war, like most Italians, and how daring we were to attack airfields like this. When he launched into a friendly chat about the job I told him to take a running poke at a rolling doughnut. That annoyed him and he asked me if I was proud to have blown up a passenger train full of women and children. I was tired enough to feel delighted that at least we had copped something after all that effort, and told him that if ever he came back to 'dear old England' he would find out what had happened to English women and children under the bombs of his allies. I was marched back to my cell feeling very pleased with myself, but that night I was roughed up by a couple of guards who barged in after dark. I suppose it made them feel better.

Next day I discovered that two more of our men, Richards and Macmillan, were in the same jail. I managed a few words and told them to sit tight. Why escape on Sardinia? The Eyeties bundled us all on a lorry later that day and took us on a tour of the local jails picking up more of our men. By the time it fell dark there were nine of us and we had plenty to talk about as we bounced and jolted through the night. The fact that we were handcuffed and chained together didn't seem to matter.

We ended up in Villegrande, or rather at an old prisoner of war camp outside the town. It was a dump. Even
in our state we turned out better than the guards, most
of whom were a sort of local home guard, I think. They
didn't have a complete uniform between them except
for the officers and one NCO. They did have rifles,
though, and we were careful to treat them with due
respect. The hut we were put in was filthy and we spent
our first two days cleaning it out. The latrines were
even worse, if that was possible, and I complained
about them when I went to complain about the rations
we were being given. The Commandant told me that if
we cleaned the place up we would get extra rations, so
we set about it. That night he sent in a turnip, ten
carrots and a bag of mouldy spuds. I threatened a
strike, but he threatened to halve the next day's rations,
so I backed down. Even a mouldy spud is better than no
spud at all.

The rest of our men were brought in on the third day
at Villegrande, and what a reunion that was. They
were underfed and prone to bouts of malaria, but still
more or less fit and ready for anything. Only the booze
was missing to make it a real party. I impressed on
them the general uselessness of escaping on Sardinia.
We must all be good boys until the Eyeties shifted us to
the mainland, but that wouldn't stop us making plans
and preparations for escape once we got there. I wrote
down every man's name and number, determined that
we would operate as a unit and show the Eyeties how
disciplined men behaved, even in captivity.

The trouble with the rations went on. There simply wasn't enough to live on so I asked to see the duty officer. He told me that only half the usual ration was authorized because we did no work. I pointed out that since we were not allowed out of the camp we could not work. He said he would speak to the CO.

All we could talk about, apart from the lousy grub, was why the operation had been such a mess. We had managed to do up a couple of aerodromes, but we couldn't see why we should all have been captured. On most jobs more people got away than were nabbed, but this time it had been a clean sweep. Malaria hadn't helped, but why was this job so different? Richards and Hannah told me they had lost touch with the South American who was with them as interpreter soon after they landed from their parachute drop. He said he had been caught on the eighth or ninth so it couldn't have been him who had blown the gaff, as some men were inclined to think.

About a week later the camp interpreter gave me a list of all our names showing how much money each man had to come. From the day of their capture, Sergeants and above were entitled to pay of one and a half Lire a day, other ranks one Lira. Much more interesting to me than the cash was the date on which each man had been captured, and the first name on the list was Louis Tronche. He'd been picked up on 3 July, the very day we had lost touch with him on the other side of the island, so it had to be him who had spilled the whole plan and got the rest of us nicked.

I had quite a job to keep the peace. Tronche was already well in with the CO, who made it very clear that whatever happened to Tronche would happen to me shortly afterwards. I told the men to leave him alone. I am sure he would have got nothing more than he deserved but there was no proof of anything. He took to following me about like a tame dog.

Some time around the middle of August the thing I had long been expecting happened at last. I had my first dose of malaria, in bed and totally helpless for five days, and weak as a kitten for weeks afterwards. Our medical orderly, Kilby, teamed up well with the Italian camp medic and worked wonders. Kilby was marvellous, nothing was too much trouble even though he was often ill himself and had very little in the way of medicine or dressings. From now on the dates and places get a bit hazy because I was often delirious and cannot clearly remember what happened when. It was around this time that we enjoyed a two-day truck ride to Port Maddelena at the northern tip of Sardinia, where we were turned out into a large tumbledown shed somewhere near the docks.

Another bunch of local home guards were in charge. They were dead scared of us even though we were on our best behaviour. You only had to raise your voice and the poor chaps would tremble and back away, clutching their rifles tighter still. Their Sergeant was made of sterner stuff, but then he was the only one with a complete uniform.

After a few days we were marched aboard the Italian

destroyer *Ardito*, and once again I have to say what a fine bunch of people sailors are. The Eyetie matelots took one sniff of us and within minutes there were razors, toothbrushes, hot showers and more than enough soap to wash ourselves and our clothes. After all the weeks of filth it was wonderful. Our home guard escort came aboard with us and seemed quite content for this to go on, except the Sergeant. He wouldn't let us go anywhere near the ship's side, once clobbering me with his rifle butt when I tried it. I was weak enough to fall down but before he could kick me a couple of the sailors grabbed him and laid him on his back. The destroyer Captain, one of the nicest Italians I met, sorted him out good and proper and we didn't see much more of him.

Most of us had galloping dysentery during the few days we were on board. The food was fine and there was plenty of it but eating hearty after weeks of going without made our insides turn somersaults. This turned out to be a blessing in disguise when we found out our officers were on board. A guard had to escort us to the heads, but before long I was setting up relays of meetings with Captain Verney to discuss tactics over the partition between the seats. We pieced together the details of the whole job and had a fair idea of the success it had been. Captain Verney confirmed that Tronche had been the traitor and asked me to take special care of him. The men were already cold-shouldering him but it was awkward. The Eyeties had treated him as our interpreter ever since we left Villegrande, because of his fluency in Italian, and the whole thing depended on him at the moment.

The docks at Naples had been put out of action by American bombing so we were put ashore nearby, but I cannot remember where. I made a point of parading the men on the dockside with bags of bull and marched them away with a smart eyes right to the destroyer Captain, a salute that he returned. Our officers were taken away somewhere else and we didn't see them again. We went to Rome by train and had to change stations, crossing the city in an open lorry. That turned out to be a good tour of all the sights with the guards happy to point them out for us. We slept that night in the bus station at Porto St Giorgio and next morning were taken to Servigliano.

This was Prisoner of War Camp 59. It contained a whole battalion of American infantry, a thousand or so men all captured in one go in North Africa, plus about two hundred British servicemen, mostly soldiers or sailors. We were lectured by the CO and told to behave, then escorted through the main gates. A whole mass of British prisoners moved forward to greet us as they opened and in front of them all was Sergeant Bill Moss, who had been captured some months before on an SBS job in the Dodecanese.

The camp looked like being my home for the rest of the war. Long rows of timber huts surrounded by a high stone wall were built around a wide central yard that served as a parade ground. There were two gates in the wall. One was the main entrance where we had come in, the other a much smaller opening at the opposite end that led on to a playing field surrounded by a barbed wire fence. The guards were elderly Italian regulars who lived in billets in the village.

It was good for the first few days just wandering around settling in, getting used to the routine and so on, with no pressure and meeting quite a few people I knew. Even so we were all thinking of escape, which was easier to think about than to do for two reasons: we were weak with underfeeding and malaria, while the guards were hard-nosed professional soldiers who knew every dodge and stood no nonsense.

There was also a third reason. The Americans were the vast majority of the prisoners, and their NCOs had formed a sort of organising committee that I was invited to join as the senior British NCO. This committee virtually ran the place in close consultation with the Italian CO, and long before we got there they had decided that escaping was a mug's game. Cooperation worked well enough in so far as the grub was plentiful, the hot water was hot, the sports field was in daily use, Red Cross parcels arrived regularly and so on. The Yanks had it all worked out: we were all going to quietly wait here for the end of the war.

One afternoon I had a terrible headache and lay down on my bunk for a kip. I woke up a couple of days later in the camp hospital. Malaria again. They told me it had taken eight of them to carry me there while I was delirious and fighting mad. I felt better after four days but very weak. A lot of us were in the same boat and

110

there could be no escaping in this condition, so we had to be patient – but we could prepare. We organized sports, PT, drill and lectures, brushing up on navigation and survival techniques. The SBS paraded as a unit for the regular roll calls and we tried to keep together as much as possible so that when a chance came to get out we would be able to make the most of it.

One morning at roll call parade we were told that an armistice had been signed between the Allies and the Italians. All hell broke loose and we spent the next few days expecting Allied troops to arrive at any minute. The CO seemed as pleased about the armistice as we were, most Italian hearts had never really been in the war, but all the same he had no orders and would not let us go. He invited the organising committee to help him run the place as his allies, but we were in fact still his prisoners. Nothing had really changed.

Our committee did decide that if we had to leave in a hurry the main gate would not be big enough, and the CO gave permission for the gate to the playing field to be widened 'a little'. I volunteered the SBS for the job and by the time we had finished he had a gateway any Commandant would be proud of. It was only about three times the agreed size. The guards blocked this gaping hole with rolls of barbed wire for the sake of appearances while the rumours kept flying. The Jerries were coming, the Allies were coming, not one of us knew a thing and the guards were still very much up to their job.

During the evening of 14 September a rumour went round that the Jerries had taken over Camp 53, which was only a few miles away. This one was taken seriously. Life hadn't been too bad under the Eyeties but we all had a fair idea of how things would change if Jerry was the boss. The whole place was in confusion for the next couple of hours as everyone packed their kit and milled about on the parade ground like sheep.

There just had to be a chance to escape in this total disorder, so I got my lot together and told them to be ready to move. The best way out would be through our new 'gate', across the playing field and over the back fence, the direct route to the hills and mountains beyond, so that was where the SBS gathered, waiting for the chance when it came. The entire guard had turned out with bayonets fixed, looking nervous and uncertain for the first time since I had been there. There was never any love lost between the Germans and the Italians and I think the guards were more scared of Jerry than they were of us. But they had their duty to do and despite the jokes we all made about Eyeties these were not the kind of men to shirk it.

Things were getting tense. Freddy Gill was not a man to stand idle when something needed doing. 'Oh, bugger this!' he said and walked towards the barbed wire rolls blocking the gate. A sentry on the wall shouted down to him, so Freddy stopped, looked up, told him where to stick his bayonet and started walking again.

The sentry cocked his rifle and fired into the air. By this time Freddy was already using a stick to drag the wire out of the way. A couple more sentries came running along the wall in response to the shot, and one of these new arrivals, thinking fast, cocked his rifle and fired as well. Sadly, he forgot to look where it was pointing and hit his mate, the man who had fired first. This poor bloke did a graceful dive off the wall and landed in the compound.

We were still taking this in when the public address crackled into life and an order was rapped out in Italian. Most of us had picked up a few words by now and worked it out as an order to cease firing and allow the prisoners free passage. The sentries still on the wall promptly forgot us and rushed down to see to their mate. We gave Freddy a hand with the wire, tore down the fence round the playing field and kept on walking. I found out much later that a British Sergeant had broken into the office, grabbed the microphone and given that order. He saved a nasty situation from getting worse.

All my men were together except for Pat Scully, who had been left behind in Sardinia too ill to travel, Wilson, who had been in another hut and didn't join us as arranged, and my old oppo Noriega who was ill with malaria again in the camp hospital. The rest of us marched most of the night, heading inland for the mountains with half the Americans trailing along behind us. They knew we had our escape maps and compasses and were just tagging along in the hope that we knew where we were going. It was no good, so in the small hours I told my men to split up in twos and threes. Choose your best pals, everybody take a different route and make your own way south east. I teamed up with Corporal Hannah, Private Hand and Ginger Farmer.

Too many scrapes and near misses happened to remember them all. After a few days it was obvious that Jerry wasn't going to break his neck recapturing us, but if we happened to walk into one of their patrols or road blocks they wouldn't object. It paid to be careful. There wasn't much to eat but we kept going up into the mountains that run the length of Italy, and the higher we got the fewer Jerries there were.

We had just about had enough when we walked into a tiny village called Meschia on 22 September or thereabouts, and were welcomed with open arms. The RC padre and the villagers soon organized who was going to put us up. Once we were comfortable they gave us an even bigger shock, because hiding out in the village and on the run from the Jerries just like us was an Italian Lieutenant.

We spent two months here. The families that kept us couldn't do enough for us, and when we were fitter we were able to help them out with the heavier jobs around the farms. All their young men had been called up years before and there were any number of lonely young ladies anxious for a bit of young male company. The boys spent all day out on the hills minding the goats, and had an efficient warning system if ever a German patrol looked like paying us a visit. The whistle went round the hillside and we were hidden with what seemed like hours to spare before we even heard their trucks grinding up the road.

We were safer in Meschia than we had been for years and it was a lovely feeling. Many times we decided we ought to move on and get back to the war, and even packed our kit. But I had a bout of malaria again, Paddy Hannah had a nasty dose of pneumonia, and all the time the idea was in the back of our minds that British troops would turn up any day now. So we didn't try too hard, it must be said.

It wasn't until 24 November that Ginger and I decided once and for all to push on. Paddy had recovered from his pneumonia but was still too weak to move, so Hand stayed with him. Ginger and I had exchanged most of our uniforms for civvies and had also picked up a fair bit of Italian. We thought we looked and sounded enough like Eyeties to pass unnoticed but I believe the only people we fooled were each other. Whenever we met any Eyeties and started talking their first question was always, 'English or American?' Happily the Jerries never took a second glance, we passed many on foot and in vehicles and not one ever stopped or spoke to us.

It was snowing in the mountains and raining in the valleys and the next few days were mostly dead miserable without having to worry about Jerries as well. We walked around the west side of the Apennines, right round the Gran Sasse, crossed the Pescara river close to Scafa and ended up near Mannopelia on 1 December, Ginger's birthday. Here we came across Benny de Primo, a former American citizen who had been deported from the States for peddling moonshine during Prohibition. He may have been a rogue but he was our best friend just then, because the weather had clamped down and we were cold, wet, tired and hungry. He led us to a disused asphalt mine where he already had a dozen other escaped PoWs hidden in the tunnels. Local farmers were sheltering their cattle there as well, so the place was filthy.

Benny kept us well fed with grub he scrounged from his neighbours – that's what he told us at any rate – and Ginger and I got really lousy for the first time, but at least it was warm and dry. On the 20 December we decided to have a crack at getting through to our lines, and one of the other men, an American pilot called Bill Glasgow, came with us.

It was a stiff climb up the Maiella in the dark, skirting round several German positions and having a nasty fright when a German staff car roared past us on the track. We climbed up to the snow line then contoured round the summit to the south eastern side. Ginger's boots fell apart on the rocks and we had to wrap his feet in whatever rags Bill and I could spare. Late the next afternoon we came to a deserted village called Pennepiedemonte, I think. There was some heavy artillery flying about and the crackle of small arms not far away as we worked our way carefully between the empty houses. The last road before the open fields contained a few Jerries walking about, so we lurked in the ruins until they cleared off.

Just before it was completely dark we decided to risk it. I crossed the road first and as I jumped down the embankment on the far side I saw some Jerries further up the road. I managed to give Ginger the tip and he stayed put while I dived into a culvert. Some time later

I heard Ginger coming, then a voice calling out in Italian. A Jerry sentry had spotted him. There was a lot of talking. The sentry's Italian was about as good as Ginger's but in the end I heard them walk away together. I waited another hour or so, but there was no sign of the Yank so I pushed on alone. It was pitch dark by now and I had some bad falls crossing the fields in the dark. I hadn't eaten for a couple of days and was just about all in when I stumbled into a sheep pen and fell asleep.

I woke about midday and lay there trying to work out where our lines were. The was a lot of firing but with the echoes it was hard to decide where it was coming from. I carried on in the dark, wading a river then heading south east by the stars, knowing I couldn't go far wrong in that direction. Around ten, a village bell began to toll and I had the impression of houses on the hillside ahead of me. I hoped the place was Palomboro which, according to Benny de Primo, was occupied by the British. Then small arms fire from in front was answered by small arms fire from behind me to my left. Great. Now both sides were trying to kill me.

I skirted round the village very carefully and carried on south-east. In what must have been the small hours I hit a road heading in more or less the right direction and followed it. It was breaking daylight when I met an Eyetie leading a donkey, and this old boy told me I was now definitely behind British lines. I sank to the ground and just sat there grinning at him until he shrugged and wandered off. Some time later a jeep came along leading a couple of trucks, so I got to my feet and stopped them. A British officer climbed out with his revolver drawn, very suspicious, and you cannot really blame him. I must have looked a sight after weeks on the run, bushy beard, civvy clothes plastered with mud and still damp from that river crossing.

Then came the biggest surprise of the whole story. We had boxed each other before the war when we were both Guardsmen, and even under all that muck he recognized me. That changed the atmosphere completely. He was now Lieutenant Woods and had a Thermos flask of tea which I helped him to empty, the best I have ever tasted, then he sent me back to Battalion HQ with his despatch rider. There I was fed while my clothes dried, and placed under close arrest.

It seems there had been a lot of infiltration attempts by Jerry spies pretending to be escaped PoWs, and they weren't taking any chances with me. I was put through the first of five interrogations. Everything I said was written down. There were so many details I couldn't remember but I gave them the basic facts. After a couple of hours I was too tired to care whether they believed me or not. I was taken under escort to Brigade HQ for another interrogation and a few hours sleep, then to Divisional HQ for the third interrogation. The Field Security Police conducted my fourth interrogation, by which time I think they were fairly sure I was a British soldier and not a German spy. At least by now I was dry and fed, although my stomach was playing up.

They put me on a truck to Vasto where I spent the

night in the New Zealand hospital, then on next day to Termoli. Here, on Christmas Eve, I had a bath, shave and delouse, put on a hospital uniform and enjoyed watching my civvy clothes go up in smoke. I was examined by a doctor and declared sick, although I felt all right apart from the grumbling guts, and went by hospital train to Bari on Christmas Day.

Bari was the depot for No 2 Ex-PoW Commission, where I was interrogated for the fifth and final time, then escorted to the ablutions tent by an MP Sergeant for a shower and a shave. He then took me to another group of tents which was the Army Field Centre for recycling any useable items found on the battlefield, weapons, uniforms and so on. There I was kitted out with a second-hand battledress and a full set of clothes from underwear to greatcoat, though I refused to change my boots. They had been badly beaten, but I wasn't going to part with them while I was still breathing because I had hidden five gold sovereigns in the heels of each one before we left Philipville. The Sergeant in the NAAFI took my IOU so I could buy a razor, toothbrush, boot polish and so on. I never did redeem it, despite the gold I was standing on.

The MP Sergeant told me to parade for CO's orders at eleven next morning. I was there on time, but as it was snowing he suggested we wait in the warmest place in the camp, the Sergeant's Mess. Next thing I remember is waking up in hospital after another bout of malaria and the CO coming to see me, to explain that every returning PoW had to be positively identified, if possible.

He had contacted a 2nd SAS unit nearby where an officer claimed to know me, and as soon as I was well enough I would be taken to see him and be identified. Until then the MP Sergeant would escort me everywhere.

I was much better the next day so my minder and I set off in a jeep I know not where. After an hour's ride he pulled into the drive of a large house where they made us very welcome – 'here's a jug of coffee, sling some more logs on the fire if you feel chilly', that sort of thing. Ten minutes later I began to sweat, sure sign of another malaria bout coming on – they seemed to be happening every twenty-four hours. Then in walked Major Scratchley, whom I had last met in the desert. 'Where the bloody hell have you been, Feebery?' he shouts, placing three glasses and a bottle of brandy on the table, bless him.

That cured the sweats for an hour while we yarned. Among other things he told me that one of my men, John Scott, had come through a few weeks before. Then the shakes hit me with a vengeance. The Major and the MP wrapped me in a blanket and bundled me into the jeep. Before we drove off Sandy shoved another bottle of brandy in my hand, and I have never seen him since.

When I came to next day the MP Sergeant crashed to attention beside my bed and held out his hand. He had scrounged a couple of brass Warrant Officer's badges from his own Sergeant Major for me to wear. Up to now he had been, shall we say, brisk in dealing with me, but whenever I met him after that trip to Sandy Scratchley he would salute and call me sir. That's when I knew for sure that I was back in the Army again.

I spent nine days at Bari. I took in an ENSA show and a couple of pictures, but mostly I slept and read and shivered in hospital. They finally decided the best place for me was England, and I began the long journey through north Africa to Algiers by way of Taranto and Syracuse. I spent three days in a transit camp at Philipville, which hadn't changed a bit, just as horrible as ever, then boarded a hospital train to Algiers for the boat home.

Later, I was woken by a medical officer. The train had stopped and he told me we'd be there for a couple of hours if I wanted to stretch my legs. Then I realized we were in Constantine, where I had seen my brother all those months ago, and asked the RTO if there was any way he could find out if Bert was still around. He very kindly made a phone call, and ten minutes later Bert arrived, riding right up onto the platform on his motor bike, jumping off and actually running along towards me. I was grinning at the look on his face until he stopped short and said, 'Where the hell have you come from? You're dead!'

We had a cup of tea on the station and chatted till the train left. It seems I had been posted missing when the first Sardinia raid was cancelled. They really had written us off and the Army, efficient in some things at least, had notified my parents. They had written to tell Bert, so he had the shock of his life when he was told to get down the station sharpish because his brother was waiting for him. It made me think while I was hanging around yet another transit camp in Algiers. I wasn't prepared for Bert's reaction. I hadn't given any thought to what the family had been told, and all I wanted to do now was to get home, back to Vera, and get rid of this flaming malaria just as quickly as I could. I landed at Liverpool on 8 February 1944.

Chapter Twelve

The End

After about a month in hospital I had got over the worst of the malaria. I took drugs that helped to keep it under control, but it was years before it cleared up completely. Vera and I got married when I came out of hospital.

1st SAS units were parachuted into France in early 1944, long before the D-Day landings, to operate alongside the Maquis and other resistance groups attacking communications, airfields, dumps and similar targets. When I was fit, Tommy Langton contacted me from 1st SAS Regiment which was then based at Darvell in Scotland, and I was posted there to work with him as Squadron Sergeant Major, HQ Squadron. Tommy's health never recovered from his African ramble, so at the age of twenty-five we were already a pair of old crocks putting keen young volunteers through their advanced training.

By August 1944, A, B and C Squadrons had been operating in France for six months or more and needed reinforcements, and I was given the job of delivering thirty men. We moved south to Fairford, and I made my first and only parachute jump in action on the night of 25 August 1944 from a Stirling bomber over Dijon. As I drifted down I wondered, briefly, what Gamp Miers and the other submariners I knew would say if they could see me now. I landed and bundled up my parachute and the first person I met was Padre McGlusky, the 1st SAS Padre who had dropped into France with A Squadron in June, who strolled out of the bushes saying, 'Ah, so you made it safely, Sergeant Major!' We shook hands then helped to find all the kit. Other friends of mine were not nearly so polite, with comments starting from, 'It's about bloody time you did something useful!' and going rapidly downhill.

It was getting light when we drove off in the convoy of Maquis lorries that had come to collect us. The French Maquis, named after the vicious thorn bushes that infest that part of the world, were grim fighters. They had given up everything for the chance to kill Jerries and some of the reprisals taken against their homes and families were horrific. Even so, I know of only one case where SAS troops were betrayed by the French in all the months they were there. It's also worth saying that there are more monuments and memorials to SAS soldiers in France than anywhere else on earth.

Our camp was in woodland near a river and very pleasant it was. We arrived in time for breakfast, after which my party of reinforcements settled into tents made from camouflaged parachutes. Things were certainly being done in style. I knew the RAF was making regular supply drops of food, fuel, explosives and ammunition, and I knew the military results that had been achieved so far, but it is one thing to sit in a cosy office in Scotland reading about it, and quite another to see it for yourself. Only then can you grasp what it's really all about.

This was the first operation for the men I had come with. After three days in camp they were fed up with being kept hanging around. Most of them were only eighteen or nineteen and they were itching to get on with it. They saw me as a doddering old fool, Sergeant Major or not, because they thought I wouldn't let them. 'Check your gear, study your maps and bide your time', I said. 'We needed to acclimatise', I said, 'and get used to being a very long way from home and surrounded by some very twitchy Jerries'. 'Get used to that first', I told them, 'you'll see plenty of action'.

That's what I told them, but I knew different. The real trouble was, nobody wanted us. The men who had been there doing it for months on end knew and trusted each other. They were, after all, the survivors, and none of them had either the time or the inclination to teach a bunch of wet-behind-the-ears newcomers how to stay alive. My reinforcements were going to be a liability until they had seen some action, but nobody was going to risk their neck showing them any action. They didn't actually say we were a bloody nuisance, but we were. It was understandable, I had been there myself, but still an awkward situation.

One important part of the SAS's task in France was gathering intelligence. Reports of German troop movements and supply convoys along the roads and railways through our area were wirelessed daily to England. It was important work but not the sort of thing that many of the old hands wanted to do, so it became the ideal job for my reinforcements. Of course it was beneath us, it was undignified and trivial because nobody else wanted the job, but for a while my thirty men raised road watching to a fine art. On the principle that if a job's worth doing it's worth doing well, roads were never before watched so carefully nor enemy movements recorded with such accuracy.

I remember once sitting in the bushes on a hillside, clipboards and pencils at the ready, enjoying the sunshine and recording activity on the road just below and the railway station beyond. Jerry never moved important trains in daylight because our aircraft would beat up every train they saw, so imagine our surprise when we heard a locomotive chuffing towards us and obviously working very hard indeed. As it came in sight there didn't seem to be any good reason for it to be working so hard because it was only pulling three long wagons. It eased into a siding at the station and Jerries swarmed over it with camouflage nets.

Three things occurred to us: the train must be very heavily loaded; the Jerries were taking the risk of moving it in daylight so it must be very important to them; it must therefore be a *very* desirable target. We wrote down the details, and a couple of men drove the jeep back to the wireless to get them sent off as fast as possible. When they came back they said the brass had been tickled pink. We later learned that they'd been keeping tabs on this train for a day or two, following its progress from traffic reports like ours, but they had lost it that morning. An immediate air strike was being organized, so we settled down for a grandstand view until someone pointed out that we were a perhaps a touch close. We retired to a more discreet distance in good time before aircraft engines roared and a flight of Typhoons came in, plastering the station and the train with rockets and cannon fire. The noise was incredible and the train was still burning when our relief took over at dusk.

Major Blackman finally got fed up with finding us little jobs to do with A Squadron and sent us to 'reinforce' Major Welstead at B Squadron. When I reported to him, he looked us over with a very long face, and I knew exactly what he was going to say.

'You're no bloody use to me!' he said. Right again, I was thinking, but then he went on, 'Why don't you go and make a nuisance of yourselves somewhere else? Go out and maraud or something!'

Now that was a bit different! Thirty trained but inexperienced men had been ordered to go and make a nuisance of themselves, so we did. This was our chance to show what we could do, so my reinforcements became 'Feebery's Marauders' and we were virtually independent for a few weeks, setting up our own camp and scrounging any gear we needed from whatever the

Big Boys didn't want. We had to make do with vehicles that were the worse for wear after heavy parachute landings. The front wheels of one jeep leaned at a crazy angle where the bearings had bent but it was still a runner. Each jeep was heavily armed, usually with Vickers K guns and Brens, while we also carried our personal weapons and a stock of ammunition, grenades and explosives in trailers. They were lethal machines, concentrated mobile firepower.

To begin with I usually went out with six men in two jeeps so as to work with a few men at a time and do some intensive on the job training. The Germans tended to stick to the main roads and we felt safe enough openly driving around the back doubles in British uniform. The Michelin maps were excellent and we learned a lot about the area we were working in, often taking a couple of Maquis along for a ride to point out landmarks, good ambush spots and so on. I remember one place vividly, where a minor road came out of the hills, ran parallel with and overlooked the main road for some distance then curved back into the hills again, ideal hit and run country.

We had parked on the verge of the minor road for a smoke and a chat about the best places to conceal weapons and so on, when along the main road about a hundred yards below came the most amazing sight. Riding along without a care in the world, with rifles slung on their backs, jingling and rattling and calling out and laughing and joking, came about 200 German soldiers on bicycles.

The End

It was almost too good to be true. We heard them long before we saw them which gave us a few seconds to get into cover and prepare. Our Brens and K-guns completely ruined their day; it only needed one or two at the front to fall off to create a pile-up of bikes and bodies which we raked. It was a nasty mess, but even so some of them were firing back before we left them to shovel it up.

Motor cyclists were also easy targets. Most of them were despatch riders and it was always worth knowing what they were carrying. We would rig a wire across the road tied off to trees or fence posts, leaving it slack so that ordinary traffic drove over it. When we heard a motor bike coming the wire would be strained tight about a yard above the ground. The bike would stop but the rider wouldn't, we would nip out of the bushes, take his pouch, then off and away.

All this driving around and road observation gave us a fair idea of the routines of local Jerry garrisons, when they were relieved and resupplied and so on. One of the first jobs for which the Big Boys needed some of my reinforcements was an ambush on one of these night supply convoys. Brens manned by 'Marauders' and the Maquis were sited on both sides of the road near a suitable bend, with plenty of cover to blaze off a few magazines and get away in the smoke. My job was to stop the leading truck as it rounded the bend, so blocking the road and giving the Bren gunners a standing target.

I had a new toy for this, an American Bazooka, an

anti-tank weapon, a long tube which fired a rocket propelled bomb over about fifty yards. It needed a two man crew, one to load, one to aim and fire, and was expected to make a nasty mess of a truck. Bob Francis and I practised the drill until we had it off pat, then got into our chosen position by the road. The tube would normally be held over the shoulder with the free hand steadying it, but because of the slope at the place we had chosen I had to lie alongside it supporting the business end on my boots. We had to be careful of the other end, too, because the rocket flame spat out a good ten feet when it fired off.

We heard the trucks growling up the hill in low gear, then the leading truck nosed round the bend and I fired. Sadly I hadn't allowed for the fact that this was a rocket, not a shell, for as it left the tube it zoomed up into the air, shaving over the top of the first truck and slamming into the cab of the second which was just turning the corner. Bob was busy reloading and thumped me on the head when he had done the necessary. Fortunately for us, the first driver had slammed on the anchors when my first shot parted his hair, then he and his mate baled out into the woods – my kind of soldiers, I hope they made it! – leaving me with a target even I couldn't miss.

The first truck went up in flames about half a minute after it should have, Brens were hammering away, grenades were going off and several fires were burning, so it seemed like a good time to leave before any resistance could organize itself. We collected everybody at the rendezvous, contacted the rearguard and drove home, where the Padre had the kettle on as usual.

Another job was to recce towns and villages to pick up whatever information we could about enemy vehicles or troop movements. Jerry rarely moved in daylight which made it even easier for us, and we were able to range far afield seeking targets of opportunity. The locals usually welcomed us with open arms in most of the places we went to, thinking we were the advance guard of the liberating armies. They all listened to the BBC and usually knew better than we did what was going on in Normandy and western France. The liberating armies were several hundred miles away, but the best wine in town flowed freely for an hour or two before we had the heart to disappoint them – and such wine! This was Burgundy!

We were parked in the bushes beside a road some-where, sleeping off yet another premature liberation, when a German truck roared past. We'll have that one, we told each other, and started up and roared after it, still half asleep and half cut. I was driving, straightening the curves to catch the truck, when a voice behind me said, 'Er, excuse me, Fee . . .'

Such politeness was unusual, to say the least, so I took notice. 'What's up?' I said, over my shoulder.

'Well, it's just that there's another two trucks behind us!'

There were no mirrors on the jeep, no glass at all for fear of reflections, so I had to look round. Sure enough, we were pounding along the main road in broad daylight in the middle of a German convoy. Bob Francis did some frantic map reading – where's the next side road? – and while he was doing that I overtook the truck we had been chasing. The couple of dozen Jerries in the back watched us go by without turning a hair.

There wasn't a junction for miles and to make matters worse we were going the wrong way. Not to worry. We were some distance ahead, so I simply made a u-turn to drive sedately back the way we had come, but this time with weapons uncovered, cocked and manned. The three German lorries, all carrying troops, passed us and went on their way taking no notice. It was better for them if they simply didn't see us.

One farm we visited turned up a real gem: a beautiful Buick saloon car, all chrome fenders, leather seats, whitewall tyres and automatic transmission. The farmer had shoved it into the barn when war broke out and there it had stood ever since because he couldn't get petrol for it. It was still a runner, so I gave him an official chit, explaining that his car was being commandeered for military purposes. When the area was liberated by the Allies he could show his chit and claim compensation.

The Buick was my 'official' transport for a couple of months while Bob followed in the jeep. We sold it several times in various places to various Frenchmen, usually the local black market operator because he was the only one who could raise enough spot cash. We'd watch to see where he parked it then steal it back and drive away into the sunrise. Incidentally, Bob went to see the farmer after the war. He had presented my chit to the Americans who liberated him and was paid a very fair price for his car, so we all ended up happy.

Speaking of markets we always had a lot of parachutes cluttering up the camp from the regular supply drops. From time to time we would load the Buick with parachutes and maybe some canned food, drive to a market in a nearby town, park up, open the boot and start trading. Most of the girls would turn cartwheels for a single panel, let alone a whole chute, and white ones were especially prized. The word quickly got around and women would soon be queuing with all the sort of stuff the RAF didn't drop, wine, brandy, eggs, milk, fruit, vegetables and so on, ready to swap for a chute or a tin of Spam. Who says boot fairs are a new idea? If any Germans turned up the locals would tip us off and we would stand out of sight in a doorway until they had gone.

All this might give the impression that this whole operation was one long jolly, a summer holiday in France which was a laugh a minute. But we knew we were deep in enemy territory, and the Germans could be very nasty if they cornered us or we pushed them too far. They made many attempts to surprise our camps, none of which succeeded because we were very much on the alert the whole time. It's just that when you are young and living on your nerves, one way to ease the tension is laugh and take the mickey and muck about, always to see the funny side of things to prove how cool and calm you are. But just let a twig snap in the woods . . .

With the Allied breakout from Normandy our operations were moving further and further east to stay ahead of the rapidly advancing Allies, or, if you prefer it, to stay behind the rapidly retreating Germans. We took Padre McGlusky to Paris to meet Berger, the chief of the Paris Maquis, while the Germans were evacuating the city, then pushed into Belgium ahead of the Canadians. We would shift camp every couple of days looking for targets and collecting information as we went.

I must mention love's young dream. Bob Francis spoke fluent French, so he had ridden with me most of the time because I didn't. One night during this time of frequent movements, he asked if he could borrow the jeep to go and see a young lady. I didn't see why not. He had lived in France for years as a boy before the war and apparently had girlfriends all over the country. Over the next few days it became a regular thing. He would drive away in the evening and be back ready to move on next morning, and I didn't question it. Good for him, it was none of my business, although he took a lot of ribbing.

It was some time before I fell in with what was really going on. Bob didn't have a girl in every town as I had thought. He was actually visiting the same girl every night, and she lived way back where we had started from. As we moved further north and east, his amorous nightly drive south and west was getting longer and longer, until he was covering hundreds of miles each time. Talk about stamina – and all behind enemy lines.

With the invasion of Germany looming, and shortly

after the liberation of Brussels, Paddy Mayne held a briefing in Louvain about the future use of SAS troops and tactics. I don't remember much about it because a bout of malaria hit me out of the blue and I woke up in hospital. I was pretty sick for a few days, so much so they decided to fly me home.

My shooting war ended almost exactly where it had begun nearly six years earlier. I landed at Northolt late at night, drugged to the eyeballs. The other five passengers were all senior officers so I kept quiet. We walked into a hut, identified ourselves, and were invited to sit while we waited for transport, but one Colonel made a hell of a fuss. He wobbled on for ages about being kept waiting, he had important business, the delay was intolerable and so on. He pounded the desk all red in the face, while the poor old RAF Sergeant had to sit there and let him. Some of the other officers joined in, agreeing with him. For me it was warm and cosy after six months in a jeep, so I was trying to get some sleep when the door crashed open and a Corporal bounced in yelling, 'Jeep for Sergeant Major Feebery!'

The Colonel had a fit. He obviously knew the SAS badge and started on me. 'Bloody jeep for you? Where's my transport? Preference for you people every time!'

'I hadn't noticed it, sir,' I said, leaving him to enjoy his nervous breakdown. There was loud welcome from the jeep and we roared off to Chelmsford where the SAS was now based. I was ready for bed, but several pals invited me in to inspect the Sergeant's mess. While we were having a drink and catching up with the gossip a voice I knew well called from the doorway.

'Is Sergeant Major Feebery in there?'

'He is,' I said, 'who wants to know?'

'Say "sir" when you talk to me! Can I come in?'

It was John Scott, last seen in the hills behind Servigliano prison camp, then a Sergeant in the SBS, now a brand new Second Lieutenant on his way to Belgium. I certainly wasn't going to bed now, and we shared a bottle and talked for hours. He won the Military Medal for the work he did in Sardinia and deserved it.

With the right drugs the malaria was soon under control again, but although I felt fine the doctors said I wasn't fit to go back to the war. I worked at Chelmsford as Regimental Sergeant Major, 1st SAS Regiment, so the office work got me in the end!

We had always got on well with the Royal Air Force, even though most aircrew couldn't understand why anyone would volunteer to jump out of a perfectly serviceable aircraft while it was still airborne. They usually treated us as being friendly but loony and perhaps they weren't far wrong. They certainly did their job by keeping us supplied and supported in France. They used Stirling and Halifax bombers to make supply and parachute drops, machines that were now obsolete for bombing missions, being far too slow, but that could still lift large amounts of supplies and personnel. They were very useful as long as Jerry didn't attack them. One evening an RAF officer turned up at Chelmsford and was sent to me by the Adjutant. Could he please borrow eight trained parachutists overnight? They wouldn't have to jump, he said, but they were needed to help check the gear for people who were jumping and give them a bit of confidence before they left. Sounded fair enough, so I rounded up some volunteers and went along to find out what it was all about.

The RAF truck dropped us at a hut on Stansted airfield, and inside there was tea on the go, books, a gramophone, armchairs, nice warm stove, all the comforts of home. It was about eight in the evening and the officer told us to make ourselves comfortable, we would be sent for when needed. A couple of hours later an RAF Sergeant looked in and asked for one of the men. We could hear aircraft engines starting up all around, and every few minutes the Sergeant would come back for another soldier until I was alone in the hut wondering what to do next. Several aircraft had taken off when the officer who had asked for us in the first place came in, looking a bit flustered.

'Would you mind helping us out, Mr Feebery?' he said. 'I'm sorry to have to ask, but I'm afraid we rather misjudged the number of your chaps we'd need.' I didn't mind at all because by now I was burning to find out what was going on. The officer explained while we were driven to an aircraft dispersal. A group of people were to parachute over enemy territory and I was to go along to help as dispatcher. My men were now all in the air with other groups for the same reason. 'Don't worry about the drill,' the officer told me, 'the rear gunner will put you straight.'

The rear gunner, an RAF Sergeant, helped me aboard a Stirling that was sitting there with the engines ticking over. He lifted a phone off the wall and spoke into it, the engines roared and we began to roll. I found somewhere to sit while the plane taxied and took off. I was in quite a big space that I took to be the bomb bay. There were eight other people, dressed in overalls, and three packing cases about two or three times the size of a tea chest. I tried to get chatting, as you do, but it soon occurred to me that most of these people couldn't speak English.

Once we were airborne, the gunner came back and began to explain. We had about an hour to go to the drop zone, during which time we had to check on the parachute harness of each of these people and make sure they were properly fitted. That was easy enough, so I took my time and did it properly with lots of nodding and smiling. Then I settled down again while we flew 'somewhere in Europe'.

The Sergeant appeared again after some time and gave me a safety harness to put on. This was a webbing belt with a length of webbing attached to it, the end of which clipped into a ring in the side of the aircraft. While I was sorting myself out he organized the people into two groups of four standing along each side of the fuselage. He gave me a thumbs up, spoke into the phone, and a huge rectangular hole yawned in the floor as the bomb bay doors opened. It got very loud and breezy and it was sign language all the way.

Between us we lowered a thick steel bar from clips in

the roof. One end was hinged to the floor, and we lowered it so the other end poked out about ten feet below and behind the aircraft. A cross piece was welded to the outer end making a T shape, the idea being that the parachute static lines would slide along to the cross piece and pull the pack clear of the chute. By that time the body underneath the parachute should be well clear of the plane. It looked neat and simple.

The Sergeant locked the bar in place with a pin and held up five fingers, which I correctly took to mean five minutes to go. The jumper's static lines were clipped to the bar and double checked with my smiling and nodding routine again. Four would jump, the Sergeant and I would shove out the three boxes, then the last four would follow. He had already hinted that some of them might need to be helped out but I was used to that. The final half minute seemed to last a year as we all stood there staring at a dim red light on the far wall. When it went green they would jump.

The light changed and the first four jumped, no panic, no hesitation. We slid the boxes out after them and the next four went, good as gold. It took a few seconds. Suddenly there was just me and the Sergeant staring at each other across this draughty room while the parachute packs flogged against the fuselage outside. A crank handle dragged them back to where we could reach them and stow them out of the way, then he phoned the pilot and the doors closed.

The Sergeant produced a flask of coffee, and while we shared it he told me that none of those people had ever made a parachute jump before, not even in practice. That was the first and probably the last time any of them would ever do it. It didn't take a genius to realize they were probably secret agents of some sort. Sooner them than me. He took me forward to the cockpit where there was a real seat, and I settled down for the ride home.

We were circling the airfield waiting for permission to land. It was still pitch dark but I had always loved flying and was standing up to watch the pilot when he nudged me and said, 'You did get the bar in, didn't you?' I looked blank and shrugged, it was no use asking me technical questions, so he got on to the rear gunner, who soon arrived all hot and bothered to drag me back to the bomb bay. The doors were opening again and I realized what the pilot meant. We were flying along with ten feet of steel bar sticking out under the aircraft. It took a few seconds to lift and clip back into place in the roof, and the doors closed again for the last time that night. The rear gunner pulled a face at me but said nothing, and I had the distinct impression there would be fireworks after I had gone.

Back in the cockpit to watch the landing, and as we taxied to the dispersal the pilot pointed out some wrecked aircraft. 'That's what you get for trying to land with the bar out!' he said. Apparently the bar would hit the ground before the wheels, dig in hard and slam the whole plane on its nose. We were in the truck taking us back to the buildings when the pilot nodded at me and said to the rear gunner, 'Put him straight!', but I'm not that thick. I told the intelligence officer the same as everybody else, the whole trip had gone without a hitch, a piece of cake. Just as well it was still dark, though.

So that was the other end of a parachute jump. My lot were scoffing RAF breakfasts and trading insults with the aircrew and getting on famously. We were soon back at Chelmsford and tucked up in bed. I remember wondering where those people who had jumped were just then, but that didn't stop me sleeping.

With peace in Europe there were only the Japs left to fight, which would have been interesting. As the hangovers from the VE Day party cleared we began making plans to have a go at them until a more urgent job came our way. The German Army of Occupation in Norway refused to surrender. They had taken to the mountains and as far as they were concerned the war wasn't over. A fully equipped armoured division was sitting in prepared positions ready to take on all comers. Would 1st SAS please go and explain?

Paddy Mayne saw it straight away; all it took was time. Spend a few weeks sending flags of truce backwards and forwards with proof that the radio broadcasts were genuine, while also making long patrols in such strength that they would have to send strong patrols to keep an eye on them, and before you knew it they had run out of fuel. Once their trucks and tanks were immobilised it was much easier to make them see reason.

They came down and were 'processed' before being sent home. This was done in the customs huts at Bergen, where a couple of dozen at a time were shepherded in

141

carrying bags and boxes that in theory contained their personal possessions. Tables and chairs were waiting with two of our men ready to 'process' each one of them.

First they had to strip to the buff, their clothing was searched, anything found was removed and they were allowed to dress again. Bags and boxes next. Each man was allowed to keep a change of clothes, just one of everything from underpants to greatcoat and nothing more. Everything else was confiscated and you would be amazed what we found among those 'personal possessions'. The men then went straight on board the ship with no further contact with the shore, and when they had all been done they sailed for the Fatherland. Most of the loot was restored to the Norwegians. Some, it must be said, was not.

It took a few weeks to clear the Jerries out of Norway. The SAS then stayed a few more weeks waiting for further orders, and what a jolly that was. We felt we had earned a break and since it wasn't at the expense of the Norwegians, or anyone else really, we took it. Norway had been used as a rest area for German soldiers who had served on the Russian front, and the best of everything occupied Europe had to offer was taken there for them to enjoy. Believe me, we made the most of it. The German officers had done particularly well and we liberated gallons of French wine on behalf of our Allies. The grub was good too, and we gave stacks away to the locals. There were facilities for swimming, athletics, skiing, yachting, fishing, every kind of sport, you name it. I had my own motor launch and plenty of fuel, and when I wasn't swimming or fishing spent many happy hours roaring up and down fjords in brilliant sunshine.

It couldn't last. We were eventually shipped back to barracks at Chelmsford. They wanted me to take a commission but I wasn't interested. I thought about Vera and what being married really meant. Bill Mansfield, the furniture dealer I had been working for when I stormed off to join the army all those years ago, said there was a job for me if I wanted it. All things considered, I wanted it. When the time came I left the Army for good and ended up dealing antiques.

It was the right thing to do. I had seen enough destruction.

Appendix A

Statement made in support of the award of the Distinguished Conduct Medal

by Major T B Langton, MC, 1st SAS Regiment

RE: 2615284 SSM FEEBERY, CYRIL

I have known SSM Feebery since 1941 when he was a Corporal in B Battalion, Layforce.

In September 1941 he and I joined the Special Boat Section in the Middle East, and two months later we took part together in the raid led by the late Lt Col Keyes, VC (Nov 18th 41). Our task was to guide the force ashore and later to try to get them off again. Both these operations were rendered extremely hazardous by the very heavy seas running. Both times Cpl. Feebery showed exceptional courage and coolness, and spent a long time in the water retrieving boats, etc, which got washed off the submarine, and saving the men who went overboard. He and I went ashore to try to get the party off, and were capsized in the surf twice. Our boat was damaged and I lost my paddle altogether. Cpl. Feebery, when I decided to try to return to the ship, paddled us both back through the heavy surf. I have no hesitation in saying that his strength, presence of mind and courage on this occasion saved us from a nasty situation.

In the next few months Special Boat Section personnel were sent out on submarine patrols from Alexandria to be put ashore at the Commander's discretion, if opportunity arose. Feebery made eight trips on submarines which included the patrol of HMS *Torbay* for which Lt/Commander Myers, DSO, RN, was awarded the VC. All the submarine's crew received decorations on this occasion. Reports of submarine commanders on Feebery's conduct and bearing on these patrols were all excellent.

Early in June 1942 Feebery (then Sergeant) was one of a small party under Major Kealy who landed on Crete. Though no positive results were obtained, Major Kealy's report – which I read – and his story which he told me personally, reflected the greatest credit on Sgt. Feebery. Once again his courage and coolness in a difficult situation was excellent.

In August 1942 Sgt Feebery took part in the raid on Benghazi led by Lt Col David Stirling, and again received excellent reports.

When the Special Boat Section was reformed in January 1943 under Major the Earl Jellicoe, DSO, MC, Feebery was made Sergeant Major of the unit, and I have no hesitation in saying that his enthusiasm and drive played a large share in the success of the unit.

Appendix B

Statement made in support of the award of the Distinguished Conduct Medal

by Major J Verney, MC, 1st SAS Regiment

RE: 2615284 SSM FEEBERY, CYRIL

On the night of 29 June 1943, SSM Feebery was put ashore on the west coast of Sardinia from a submarine. There were two parties of five each, commanded by Capt. Thompson 2nd SAS Regiment, and Lt Duggin attached to 2nd SAS Regt, with the rest of 'L' Detachment, Special Boat Squadron, for the operation. SSM Feebery was 2nd i/c to Lt Duggin's party.

The two parties landed together at night on the coast within a short distance of an Italian port. They had not been seen, but found themselves at the foot of a high and very steep cliff, with only two hours of darkness left. Five out of the ten including Lt Duggin were in a weak state, thought at first to be the effects of the submarine trip, but which turned out to be malaria. Both officers told me afterwards that without SSM Feebery's great strength and courage they would not have climbed the cliff. He scaled it first with a rope, a hazardous task in the dark, and then made several trips up and down hauling the others and their packs to the top. They were all safely up before dawn and remained concealed the next day. The two parties spilt up then to march to their respective airfield targets.

After six days Lt Duggin and two others were too exhausted with malaria to continue. Owing to the rough going and the delay caused by their weakness, there was no hope of reaching the airfield in time. Lt Duggin told SSM Feebery and the other remaining man, Pte. Noriega, to carry on to the RV on the east coast, laying charges on a railway line which had been given to them as a secondary target if the airfield failed, en route. SSM Feebery and Noriega found the line and laid the charges, and then made for the east coast RV across country.

Unfortunately the RV had already been compromised and rounded up. SSM Feebery and Noriega reached it on 18 July after a tremendous march through enemy country over very rough and difficult going, to find Italian troops there on the lookout. I spoke later to the Italian officer who captured him, having been sent to the RV for that purpose. He knew rubber dinghies had been found on the west coast where Feebery landed, but he did not believe it possible for anyone to walk across the island in the time, and insisted that Feebery must have been dropped by parachute.

I saw Feebery a month later at Maddelena, where we were both waiting to be shipped to Italy. 25 O/Rs from the Special Boat Squadron were with him, and although they were ill from malaria and under-feeding, Feebery had them admirably under control and was keeping them both as smart and as cheerful as could have been expected. Their morale, thanks to his splendid leadership, was quite amazing, and it was amusing to note the respect the Italian guards treated them with, evidently terrified of some sudden *coup de main* by Feebery.

I was not surprised to hear that when Italy collapsed, Feebery led all his men out of their POW camp in one party and then split them up into smaller parties to make for British lines. Many have now returned safely, including Feebery himself.